A. Lincoln

A Life in the Shadow of

DEATH

Bill Kolasinski

WILLIAM KOLASINSKI

DEDICATION

To my wife and family, who, after joining me in visiting
countless Lincoln sites around the country over the past decades,
still remain willing to see more.

CONTENTS

ACKNOWLEDGMENTS

I must admit my awe of the work that has been done by so many great Lincoln scholars over the years. They have continued to inspire me with each of their new works, to learn more about that most unique of men, Abraham Lincoln. No matter how much is written about him, there is always more to discover.

I definitely need to thank my wife for her patience in helping me when my computer skills were lacking, and my daughter, Kate Doane, for her invaluable work in getting this book ready for publishing, and for her beautiful cover art. My fondest hope is that anyone who reads this book finds what is in it to be as interesting as its cover.

Lastly, I want to thank my proof readers, Gary Koca, Larry Stivers and Mary Lynne Fontaine, for keeping me humble by showing me just how little I have mastered of English grammar.

INTRODUCTION

For a good part of his adult life, Abraham Lincoln believed in the doctrine of predeterminism. It holds that every person has a part to play during his time on earth, a part that has been written for him by his Creator before his birth.

That view is not so widely embraced today as it was in Lincoln's time. We see ourselves and our lives as the result of many ingredients: familial DNA, which leaves us with physical characteristics and psychological tendencies; relations with others whose lives intersect with our own, leaving impressions on our personality; and events happening in the world we move through that change our outlook for better or worse.

So we must look at a person's family, friends, and the events he lives through to best understand him.

The Lincoln family, whose roots can be traced back to England, had a strong vein of mental instability running through it. Abraham Lincoln's great uncle once told a court judge that he was troubled by "a deranged mind. " Neighbors of the Lincoln family spoke of their mood swings, drinking, and violence, which they termed "Lincoln characteristics."[1] Abraham's uncle Mordecai suffered from severe mood swings, aggravated by heavy drinking. He was said, by those who knew him, to move frequently from melancholy to mania, showing, at times, a weak grip on reality. Abraham's first cousin had a daughter, Mary Jane Lincoln, who was committed to the Illinois State Hospital for the Insane. The jury in her committal hearing received testimony that she had suffered from a disease of the mind for thirteen years. The jury concluded that "the disease is, with her, hereditary." [2]

Thomas Lincoln, Abraham's father, was remembered by his friends and neighbors for his athletic ability, his story-telling, and his periods of depression. One Kentucky neighbor recalled that Thomas "often got the blues, and had some strange sort of spells, and wanted to be alone all he could when he had them. He would walk away out on the barrens alone, and stay out sometimes half a day." When these spells occurred, his neighbors would fear that he "was losin his mind."[3]

John Hanks stated that the character of Abraham Lincoln's mother Nancy "was kindness, mildness, tenderness, sadness." Abraham himself said his mother Nancy was "intellectual, sensitive and somewhat sad."[4] Throughout her life Nancy was tormented by local gossip that claimed that she was born illegitimate, the love child of a rich eastern land owner and one of his servants. Abraham suspected that this was true. William Herndon, his law partner and biographer, claimed that Abraham once told him:

Billy, I'll tell you something, but keep it a secret while live. My mother was a bastard, was the daughter of a nobleman, so called, of Virginia. My mother's mother was poor and credulous, and she was shamefully taken advantage of by the man. My mother inherited his qualities and I hers.[5]

Given this ancestral background, it is not difficult to understand why Abraham Lincoln developed a disposition to dark thoughts and depression.

When we examine the personal experiences of Abraham Lincoln's life, what stands out most is how many times he came close to dying, or experienced the death of those close to him. His extraordinary dance with death began at age 3, and continued to his last day. The shadow that slowly enveloped him contributed substantially to the formation of his personality and outlook on life. Add to that his ancestry, his parents' personalities, his relationship with them, the people he loved and how their life experiences affected him, and the events of the nation that unfolded as he grew to realize his potential, and we begin to see how a poor farm boy of dubious origins became the marble man seated in the Lincoln Memorial.

Let us begin at the beginning.

William Kolasinski

Chapter One

BACKWOODS BOYHOOD

In the spring of 1807, Thomas Lincoln, his wife Nancy, and their little daughter Sarah, moved to a farm in Kentucky, which they named **Rock Springs**. The family had left their tiny one room shack, located at the end of an alley in Elizabethtown, Kentucky, so that Thomas could try his hand at farming. He had been respected by his neighbors in Elizabethtown as a good carpenter, and an honest and reliable man. Standing five feet nine inches tall, weighing about 180 pounds, with broad, powerful shoulders, black hair, and dark eyes, he was a favorite at social gatherings. Men would group around him to listen as he told story after story, most with a moral or joke or both wrapped in them. He could write his name, but little, if anything, else. He took no time to read for pleasure, but did read Bible verses during family meals. His wife Nancy, according to her first cousin John Hanks, was spare of frame, with dark hair and hazel eyes, standing about five feet seven inches – tall for a woman of the time. She could read and write a bit,

and had a sad and serious, but calm temperament. Hanks thought her to be quick-witted, though without any formal education.

Thomas built a one room cabin on a rise just above the spring from which he got the name for his farm. The family could look out their one window and see the rolling hills and fields, and observe the weather that would affect the success or failure of their growing crops. The cabin had one door hung from leather hinges, and one bed hung from pegs driven into the log and mud-chinked walls. Nancy arranged their few pieces of furniture to make the space livable, and she, along with Thomas and little Sarah, scraped, pounded and stomped the ground inside to give them a flat packed dirt floor. A small fireplace provided some warmth and light, with smoke travelling up and out of the cabin from a chimney made out of sticks and clay.

A neighbor described their living conditions:

The Lincoln's had a cow, a calf, milk and butter, a good feather bed – for I have slept on it. They had home woven kidlivers (bed covers), big and little pots, a loom and a (spinning) wheel. [1]

***

Childbirth in the early 19th century was an unsettling event that filled future parents with equal measures of fear and joy. Statistics were grim. One out of every four infants born in those days died before their first birthday. [2] Doctors were few and far apart on the frontier, and midwives were typically the only medical support available to help deliver babies. In the early winter of 1809 Thomas hailed a neighbor walking past the cabin and asked the man to please go and tell "the granny woman" Aunt Peggy Walters to come quick, for his wife was ready to give birth. Thomas and Nancy Lincoln welcomed a baby boy into the world not long after Aunt Peggy arrived.

After covering his wife with an extra bearskin blanket, Thomas left the cabin and walked two miles to the home of the Sparrows. Tom and Betsy Sparrow had raised Nancy after her mother's death, and she

remained close to them and their nine year old adopted son Dennis Hanks. Thomas told them, "Nancy's got a baby boy."

The Sparrows made ready to join Thomas and his wife and provide some much needed help. Dennis Hanks, curious and anxious to meet his new relative, headed out to the Rock Springs farm with **Thomas Lincoln**. Once they arrived back at the farm, Dennis asked an exhausted **Nancy Lincoln** what she was going to name the sleeping baby. She answered "Abraham, after his grandfather." [3]

The next morning, **Dennis Hanks**, who had spent the night sleeping on the floor of the Lincoln cabin near the fireplace, stood over Nancy and the newborn baby and said "its skin looks just like red cherry pulp squeezed dry, in wrinkles." He then asked if he could hold his new playmate, and Nancy reluctantly agreed. Dennis gently swung the baby back and forth, talking all the while about the adventures they were going to have together. The baby, startled by his actions, screwed up its

face and began to wail without letup. Dennis turned to Betsy Sparrow, who had come by that morning to help with the baby, and passed him off to her saying, "Aunt, take him. He'll never come to much!" [4]

As Abe grew his mother began to teach him words. She eventually began to explain to him about where he lived, and how Kentucky was a small part of a big country called the United States. One day Thomas Lincoln stepped outside of their cabin, pointed his rifle in the air and fired it. Confused, Abe asked his father what he was doing, and Thomas explained to him that it was the Fourth of July, the day the United States became a free country. [5]

The words Abe learned from his mother were spoken in an accent and dialect unique to the Kentucky area. A man who read books was "eddicated." If you were certain of something, then you were "sartin." Joints were "j'ints." Old fruit got "spiled." Flannel was "flannen" If you got something, you "brung" it back. When you planted corn you "drapped" the seeds. If you spoke differently from this you were "puttin on." [6]

***

In 1812 joy filled the Lincoln cabin by the sunken spring. Nancy gave birth to another child, a second son, named for his father, Thomas. Abraham was excited at the idea of a new playmate. Then, just three days later, something happened.

It was very confusing and upsetting for Abraham. Neighbors were suddenly appearing at the door of their cabin, talking low so he couldn't hear, hugging his mother Nancy, and looking at him and his older sister Sarah with teary eyes. Thomas was outside, avoiding the visitors, banging and cutting, building something in a hurry. And why wasn't baby Tom fussing? Abe was jealous of all the attention his new brother was getting, but today everyone seemed to ignore baby Tom as he lay silent, all swaddled in his crib. His big sister Sarah had been quiet all morning, avoiding his questions about what was going on. When the last of the neighbors left, Nancy called Abe over to her as she stood over Tom's crib. Your baby brother is gone to God, Abe, she explained between sobs. He is gone to God. [7]

Death had paid its first visit to Abraham Lincoln. He rarely spoke of his baby brother Thomas to friends, or even his own wife, in the years to come. What impression his baby brother's death made on him when Abraham was only three years old is pure conjecture, but surely it left some mark, buried deep in his subconscious.

***

In the three growing seasons that the Lincoln's stayed at the Rock Springs farm, they were barely able to grow enough food to feed themselves. Surplus crops that could be sold for a profit were rarely achieved. Thomas decided it was time to move to better land.

The family journeyed ten miles north to a 238 acre parcel of land situated on **Knob Creek**, which began on nearby Muldrow's Hill and continued to flow down to a junction with the Rolling Fork River. This farm was well-timbered and contained some rich valley land, which promised far better growing conditions than they had at Rock Springs. After much hard work clearing six acres of land, Thomas

Lincoln began planting what he hoped would be a good crop of corn. In the few hours he could spare away from tending to his crop, Thomas also continued his work as a carpenter, fulfilling orders from neighbors for tables and chairs and coffins.

***

For a young boy growing up in Hardin County, Kentucky, adventure was just outside the cabin door. There were limestone cliffs, hidden valleys, creeks and a large pond perfect for swimming. At home Abe had his sister for a playmate, though she was often busy helping her mother with the chores that filled every pioneer woman's life. Whenever he was allowed, Abe, led at first by his older cousin Dennis Hanks, set about taking the measure of the area. They hunted ground hogs and squirrels, "shot fish in puddles and holes washed by the water," and climbed trees. Dennis Hanks said that in these years Abe exhibited a good, kind, somewhat wild nature. [8] And he was growing fast.

Carl Sandburg, in his great biography of Lincoln, wrote that Thomas kept young Abe very busy on the farm. Thomas could not abide idleness. Abe ran errands, held burning pine knots to provide lighting for his father at night as Thomas finished a carpentry order, carried water, filled the family's wood box, hoed weeds, and picked berries, grapes and persimmons for beer-making.

At age seven, Abe, sometimes accompanied by his sister, walked four miles to attend a school run by Zachariah Riney and Caleb Hazel. There was one room to accommodate all grade levels. Students learned their lessons by saying them out loud to themselves until they were ready to recite to the class. It was known as a "blab school," and was typical for that time on the frontier. Abe learned multiplication and the alphabet, but was not able to attend regularly because he was often needed at home to do chores. At age eight he was already big enough to wield an axe, and his father had him chopping wood for the fireplace and clearing brush from the fields that were to be plowed. His learning was not limited by his inability to attend school.

Christopher Columbus Graham was a frequent boarder at the Lincoln family cabin. Graham was a doctor and naturalist who studied the rocks, flowers, plants, trees, and wildlife in the region. When he stayed overnight at the Lincoln farm, he slept in Abraham's bed while Abraham slept on the dirt floor. He kept Abraham entertained with tales of what he found growing in the forests, and spun stories of the famed Kentuckian Daniel Boone, who had hunted the very woods around the Lincoln cabin. Abraham also listened in when travelling preachers would stop at their cabin to swap stories with Thomas Lincoln about the early days when church meetings were held in people's homes, often interrupted by curious local Indians wandering in. [9]

***

In Kentucky, Abraham's parents were members of the Little Mount Baptist Church. It was a rigid, fiery brand of religion, known as Hard Shell Baptists. They did not believe in anything other than the gospel of Christ; no Sunday school, no missionary work, no musical instruments at worship, and no paid or educated clergy. They did not recognize "free will," but instead believed in the doctrine of predestination. God determined daily events, and had already chosen who was to be saved. Lincoln would hear discussion and debate about these beliefs around his family's dinner table, at the local store, and all around the neighborhood. This became the basis of his first impressions of what role God played in the lives of men.

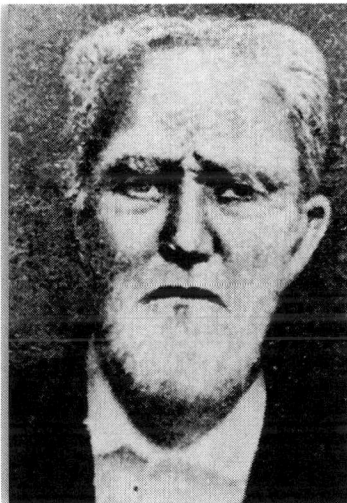

***

Abe's best friend in these years was **Austin Gollaher**, a neighbor boy of about the same age. When the two boys completed their chores they would head into the forests to hunt fish and swim until dinner time. Sometimes another neighbor boy, John Duncan, would join them. [10]

When he was an old man, Duncan told the following story to William Herndon:

... as to his hunting he was very determined in pursuit of game...him and myself on one occasion ran a Groun hog in a hole in the rocks – we worked some four or five hours in trying to git him out – I gave out. Lincoln then went off about a quarter mile to a black Smith shop and got the black Smith to make an iron hook and fasten it on a pole. The black smith went with young Abe and hooked the Groun hog out of the rocks. [11]

Charles Friend, a relative of Dennis Hanks, told Lincoln biographer William Herndon a story in 1889 about a meeting that a Hardin County neighbor, Dr. J. H. Rodman, had with Lincoln when he was President. Lincoln asked Rodman many questions about old friends from their time in Kentucky, especially Austin Gollaher. "Where is my old friend and playmate Gollaher? I would rather see Gollaher than any man living. He played me a dirty trick once and I want to pay him up." [12]

Lincoln then related the incident:

One Sunday Gollaher and another boy and myself were out in the wood on Knob Creek playing an hunting around for young squirrels when I climbed up a tree and left Austin and the other boy on the ground. Shortly Gollaher shut his eyes like he was asleep. I noticed his hat sat straight with the reverse side up. I thought I would shit in his hat. Gollaher was watching and when I let the load drop he swapped hats and my hat caught the whole load. [13]

When he finished the story the President broke into a wide grin and slapped his knee, laughing loudly.

Lincoln told friends in Washington D.C. that his first memories were of his time on the Knob Creek farm. He spoke of hunting, swimming, all sorts of boy's adventures. But he never spoke of his first personal brush with death, which occurred in the green, densely wooded hollows near Knob Creek. He again was with his friend Austin

Gollaher, who described the events of that day to another great Lincoln biographer, Ida Tarbell.

He and I had been going to school together for a year or more, and had become greatly attracted to each other...One Sunday morning my mother visited the Lincoln's and I was taken along. Abe and I played around all day. Finally we concluded to cross the creek to hunt for some partridges young Lincoln had seen the day before. The creek was swollen by a recent rain, and, in crossing on the narrow footlog, Abe fell in. Neither of us could swim. I got a long pole and held it out to Abe, who grabbed it. Then I pulled him ashore. He was almost dead, and I was badly scared. I rolled and pounded him in good earnest. Then I got him by the arms and shook him, the water meanwhile pouring out of his mouth. By this means I succeeded in bringing him to, and soon he was all right. [14]

But for the quick reaction of his friend, and the availability of a stout, long tree branch, Abraham Lincoln's life might have ended that day. Lincoln never spoke to anyone of this event in the years to come. We only know of it from his boyhood friend, Austin Gollaher. This frightening experience merged with his other childhood memories to help define the still maturing emotional makeup of the contradictory character that could shift from jovial story teller to silent, self-critical brooder.

William Kolasinski

Chapter Two

CROSSING THE OHIO

I t is not clear why Thomas Lincoln decided to move his family from their Knob Creek farm in the slave holding state of Kentucky to the free state of Indiana. Lincoln biographers William Herndon and Albert Beveridge argue that slavery had little to do with the move. They believe that Thomas Lincoln was looking for richer farmland in a state where he could obtain a secure deed to his property. In Kentucky, many settlers were losing their farms to Eastern families who hired lawyers to lay claim to large tracts of land that had been deeded to their ancestors just after the Revolution. Thomas had suffered just that kind of land loss.

Other Lincoln scholars believe that slavery was at least one of the reasons Thomas decided to move his family to a free state. Louis A. Warren cited the fact that in 1816 there were 1,238 slaves listed in the Hardin County Kentucky Tax Book.[1] One citizen in the county owned 58 slaves. The presence of slaves in Hardin County meant that those farms run with slave labor could out produce those operated by families alone. Also, the presence of slave labor reduced the opportunities for men like Thomas Lincoln to find odd jobs to work as a supplement to their farm income. More proof of the tensions created by the presence of slaves in Kentucky is found in the record book of the South Fork Baptist Church, which was two miles from the

Lincoln's Rock Springs farm. In 1808, fifteen members of that church left it because of their opposition to slavery in the area. By the time the Lincolns moved into the area that church was closed for good due to fighting amongst its flock over slavery. The Lincolns joined the Little Mount Church, a Baptist anti-slavery congregation.[2]

For a variety of reasons then, in the fall of 1816, Thomas Lincoln began building a flatboat that would carry him to southern Indiana. Seven year old Abe helped his father, carrying Thomas' carpenter's tools down from the cabin to the shore of Knob Creek where his father placed them on the boat. Their good feather bed, bed linens, blankets, a spinning wheel, a steel plow point, axe and cooking utensils were brought aboard, followed by cured meat that had been prepared during the hog-killing season, seed corn for planting and shelled corn for family consumption. Space would be tight, so most furniture was left behind. Thomas could build what they needed once they reached Indiana. One cow was brought along, to provide a source of milk, cream and butter. The last critical piece of cargo loaded was 40 ten gallon barrels of whiskey. Thomas, who was not a drinking man, had traded their farm for the whisky, which was often used on the frontier as a kind of money. He would have no trouble selling it or trading it to the thirsty inhabitants of Indiana.

***

Thomas and his family left the Knob Creek farm for Indiana sometime around Thanksgiving, 1816. The trip would be arduous, but not unusual for frontier families. They would have to cover about 100 miles of terrain, crossing streams and rivers, climbing hills, finding their way through dense growths of brush and trees. Thomas and Abe rode one horse, Nancy and Sarah the other. When the going got rough, Thomas and Nancy walked. The longer they travelled the wilder and more isolated their surrounding became. Rutted trails became paths, then, even the paths disappeared, and there were only tall grasses and thick stands of beeches, oaks, elms and maple trees. After several days they reached the shores of the Ohio River. Abe and his sister Sarah must have marveled at the sight, never having seen so big a body of water. They may even have glimpsed a passing barge or steamboat wending its way up or down river.

The Lincoln family crossed the Ohio River and entered Indiana on or about December 11, 1816, the day Indiana came into the Union as a state.[3] There were only 16 miles left on their journey, but they would be difficult ones. The Lincoln's set out following a newly cleared rough road that went from Troy, a little town near Thompson's Ferry to Hurricane Township, passing within about four miles of Thomas Lincoln's property. The trip went slowly, with the horses straining to pull the wagon loaded with all of the family's earthly goods over the rock strewn, frozen ground. When they reached the point where they had to leave the road, things got much worse. Neighbors later recalled that Thomas Lincoln "...came in a horse wagon, cut his way to his farm with an axe felling the trees as he went."[4] In a short autobiography, Abraham Lincoln later stated that he "...never passed through a harder experience than he did in going from Thompson's Ferry" to their campsite.[5]

Thomas seems to have selected a good location for his new farm. There were several sources for clean drinking water a short walk away. A salt lick was nearby, which would attract wildlife, and a canopy of oak, hickory and hazel trees would provide shade from the heat. Thomas chose the top of a small knoll near the township trace as the spot to build his new cabin. The elevation would keep the cabin area airy, dry and healthy.

Growing season was over, so the Lincolns could spend all the time they needed building their new cabin. Thomas had already built several in his lifetime, so he knew what to do and how to do it. Neighbors, aware of the new family in the area, probably joined them in their efforts. Young Abraham, aged eight, going on nine, wielded an axe, helping his father chop down trees and notch logs for the corners of their new cabin. A fellow citizen of the southern Indiana area at that time described how rapidly the work could be done.

23

Arrived on Tuesday, cut logs for the cabin on a Wednesday, raised the cabin on Thursday, clapboards from an old sugar camp put on Friday and on Saturday made the crude furniture to go to housekeeping.[6]

From this description it is fair to assume that the Lincoln family was able to enjoy their first Christmas in Indiana together sitting in front of the fireplace in their **new cabin on Pigeon Creek.**

Nine-year-old Sarah and seven-year-old Abraham were living in a frontier wilderness. Family became all important. Both parents would be the chief architects of their children's moral and intellectual growth in the years to come. Thomas could barely write his name, and did little if any reading beyond Bible verses at dinner. Nancy enjoyed sewing, singing, and reciting Bible stories to her children, but had never been taught how to write. She could read, but only in the most rudimentary manner. Dennis Hanks wrote in letters to Lincoln biographer William Herndon, of how Nancy worked with her children to educate them as best she could.

Their mother first learned them their ABC's and then AB's. She learned them this out of Webster's old spelling book...Lincoln's mother learned him to read the Bible-study it and the stories in it and all that was morally and affectionate in it, repeating it to Abe and his sister when very young.[7]

Nancy Lincoln was known by her neighbors to be a good singer, and often sang songs to her children that she had learned from her mother back in Virginia. Many times they related a strong message about proper behavior. FAIR ELLENDER was a ballad about a dark skinned bride who stabs a man that ridiculed her, only to have her head cut off by her own husband, who then kills himself. WICKED POLLY was another favorite. Polly carried on a wild life, telling her folks "I'll turn to God when I get old, and he will then receive my soul." Unfortunately for Polly, she was struck down while still young, and dying, told her Mother, "When I am dead, remember well, your wicked Polly screams in Hell."[8]

Young Abraham became the family correspondent, writing letters for his parents to friends back in Kentucky. This caused him to become the talk of the area, for at the tender age of seven, unlike nearly all other neighbor children near his age, he could both read and write. A biographer tells of how he perfected his penmanship skills.

For this acquirement he manifested a great fondness. It was his custom to form letters, to write words and sentences wherever he found suitable material. He scrawled them with charcoal, he scored them in the dust, in the sand, in the snow - anywhere and everywhere that lines could be drawn, there he improved his capacity for writing.[9]

There was much work to be done to make their farm livable and profitable. Clearing the land was the first chore. Thomas, with help from his eight year old son Abe, eventually removed enough trees and rocks from six acres to ready it for planting. Young Abe was tall for his age, and was already familiar with how to clear brush with an axe. He spent hours each day in the field with his father doing what needed to be done. According to Dennis Hanks, while he was a good boy, who loved and respected his parents, Abraham began to show a tendency to speak up before spoken to. This breach of frontier etiquette caused his father, on several occasion, to punish him. Hanks described these moments:

Sometimes Abe was a little rude. When strangers would ride along and up to his father's fence Abe always, through pride and to tease his father, would be sure to ask the stranger the first question, for which his father would sometimes knock him a rod. Abe was then a rude and forward boy. Abe, when whipped by his father, never bawled but dropt a kind of silent unwelcome tear, as evidence of his sensations – or other feelings.[10]

With the cabin built and the land cleared, Nancy, Abe and his sister Sarah began the work of planting a vegetable garden that would supply the family table. Alternating the crops seasonally, they dropped seeds for potatoes, turnips, cabbage, beets, roasting corn, pumpkins, and squash, cucumbers, eggplant and water melon. With the garden planted Nancy moved on to spruce up the outside of the cabin by planting poppies, marigolds, larkspur, hollyhock and bachelor button. These would bloom and add additional color to the sweet william, lady slipper, wild rose and butterfly weed abundant in the area.

***

Indiana in 1816 was a frontier state, with a population density of three people average per square mile, far less than the 10 people per square mile average of the Lincoln's former home state, Kentucky. But that leaves an incorrect and still widely believed impression of the Lincoln's Pigeon Creek homestead as being a lonely oasis in a vast area of uninhabited forest. In fact, the Lincoln's farm was part of a growing frontier settlement. 18 families with forty-five boys and forty-five girls under seven years of age and twenty-three boys and twenty-five girls between seven and seventeen years of age lived within a four mile radius of the Lincoln farm. Abraham met many of these children while travelling to the local mill with his father, or while joining him on his odd-jobs in the area. Once he began attending school, he met nearly all of his other neighbors. It was not, as widely thought, a lonely existence for Abraham in Indiana.

In the fall of 1817, Thomas and Betsy Sparrow, who were close to Nancy Lincoln and had been neighbors of the Lincoln family when they lived in Kentucky, travelled to the Lincoln's Pigeon Creek cabin from Hodgenville, Kentucky. The arrival of the Sparrow family was cause for great celebration. Thomas Lincoln told them they could live in the half-faced camp he had built for his own family when he first came to the area, until the Sparrows could build a cabin for themselves.

The joy of reunion between the Sparrows and the Lincolns was interrupted in the summer of 1818 by an outbreak of a feared disease, known variously as "puking fever," "river sickness," and "fall fever." Eventually it would be known as "the milk-sick," An article in an Evansville, Indiana, newspaper described the pioneer reaction to this illness.

There is no announcement which strikes the members of a western community with so much dread as the report of a case of milk sickness. The uncertainty and mystery which envelopes its origin, and its fearful and terrible effects upon the victims, and the ruinous consequences upon the valuable property, which follows in its train, makes it in the eyes of the inhabitants of a district the worst looking foe which can beset the neighborhood."

Citizens knew that cattle were somehow involved in the passing of the disease. When a person consumed milk from a cow that had "the trembles," he could come down with the illness. It was thought that the water supply in the area of an outbreak must be contaminated with arsenic, cobalt or lead leached from the minerals in the streams, then drunk by the cows, or that these poisonous minerals might, through evaporation be borne on the morning mists, to be inhaled by cows in the area. No one suspected the true cause, which was the consumption by cows, of a plant known as snakeroot. The plant's thick, fibrous roots were able to draw enough moisture from shady places to grow waist high stalks, topped with clusters of bright, white flowers. It had been an especially hot summer, and cattle were foraging in the shady areas where this plant grew in great numbers.

In the fall of 1818, Thomas Lincoln discovered that one of his cows was showing signs of the "trembles." Soon, Thomas Sparrow was stricken with the disease. The Lincolns moved the Sparrow family into their own cabin, but Thomas Sparrow died within a week. His will left all his earthly goods to his wife Betsy. Unfortunately, Betsy soon was afflicted with the milk sick, and passed away quickly, despite the efforts of Nancy Lincoln to nurse her back to health. A nearby neighbor, Mrs. Peter Broomer, also succumbed to the illness. There was no doctor within thirty miles of their Pigeon Creek cabin, and even if there had been one close by, the family could not have afforded his services.

Thomas Lincoln, aided by his nine year old son Abraham, busied himself with building coffins for his recently deceased neighbors. As Nancy Lincoln nursed the dying Betsy Sparrow, she too began to display the awful symptoms of the disease. A physician of the time described an afflicted person's suffering: When an individual is about to be taken down, a thick white coat forms on the tongue, he feels weary, trembles more or less under exertion, and often experiences pain, numbness, and slight cramps. Nausea follows, then a feeling of depression and burning at the pit of the stomach, then retching, twitching and tossing side to side. Then the patient becomes deathly pale and shrunk up, listless and indifferent, and lies, between fits of retching, in a mild coma. Nancy Lincoln fought the illness for a week, with her husband, daughter Sarah, and son Abraham, doing all they could to make her comfortable and delay the inevitable. It soon became clear that Nancy's life would not be spared. Dennis Hanks recalled the scene:

She knew she was going to die and called up the children to her dying side and told them to be good and kind to their father-to one another, and to the world, expressing a hope that they might live as they had been taught by her to live...love-reverence and worship God.[12]

On October 5, 1818, Nancy Lincoln died, at age thirty-six. Thomas, as he had so frequently in the past few weeks, whipsawed logs into planks and fashioned the coffin. Nine year old Abraham whittled the pegs used to secure the lid. The family placed the coffin on a sled and their work horse pulled it to the crest of a small hill just south of the cabin. There, under a canopy of oak, maple and walnut trees full with brightly colored autumn leaves, they buried her, next to Thomas and Betsy Sparrow, who had perished just weeks before. Field stones were placed at the head and foot of the grave, with the letters N.L. scraped into the head stone. A very simple interment ceremony concluded the burial.

The family of Rev. David Elkin (who had been the pastor at Nancy's church in Kentucky) stated that young Abraham wrote to the reverend, asking him to come and preach at his mother's grave. Reverend Elkins did, for whatever reason, travel to the area weeks after Nancy's death. At the gravesite he delivered a sermon for some twenty townsfolk gathered there. An eyewitness recalled the ceremony:

A MEMORABLE SCENE.—FUNERAL OF LINCOLN'S MOTHER.

As the appointed day approached notice was given the entire neighborhood. On a bright Sabbath morning **the settlers of the neighborhood gathered in** *Some came in carts of the rudest construction, their wheels consisting of huge boles of forest trees and the product of axe and auger; some came on horseback, two or three upon a horse, others came in wagons drawn by oxen,* *and still others came on foot. Taking his stand at the foot of the grave Parson Elkin lifted his voice in prayer and sacred song and then preached a sermon. He spoke of the precious Christian woman who had gone, with the warm praise which she had deserved, and held her up as an example of true womanhood.[13]*

It is difficult to imagine what effect the suffering and slow death of his mother might have had on a nine-year-old boy. Sharing a 15 square foot space with a grieving father and sister and convulsive, semi-comatose mother had to take a toll on the emotional health of the impressionable, sensitive boy, though it was not an unusual event in 19th century America. One fourth of all children lost a mother or father before age fifteen. Lincoln's contemporaries did not report him to be particularly melancholy before his twenty-first year. But a pattern was emerging. By age nine Abraham had lost his baby brother, nearly drowned and witnessed the slow death of his aunt, uncle and mother.

***

The death of his mother was surely painful, but what was even more difficult for Abraham was that this death left him and his sister alone with a father who saw little of value in anything beyond the most basic education. When she was alive, Nancy did her best to encourage Abraham's and his sister Sarah's education, sending them off to school twice in Kentucky for short periods of time. Thomas felt that his children had learned enough of the basics to allow them to succeed as farmers on the frontier. Any more learning would be a waste of time. Thomas Lincoln saw Abraham's growing love of reading and writing as a sign of laziness, not accomplishment, and would never fill the void left in his son's life by the death of his mother.

The family, without a mother's influence, was suffering. The cabin and its occupants began to look more and more disheveled. Abraham's sister Sarah did her best, but a thirteen year old still learning the skills of housekeeping could only do so much. Thirteen months after Nancy's passing, Thomas announced to his children that he was leaving Pigeon Creek for Elizabethtown, Kentucky, to find and bring home a new mother for them.

Thomas left his children in the care of a neighbor, Sophie Hanks, and took off for what he expected would be a three month trip. After four and then five months passed, without word from their father, Abraham and Sarah began to believe that he had fallen prey to wild animals or highwaymen roaming the trails, and thought themselves to be orphans.

Sometime during the sixth month of their bleak, lonely life in the cabin, they heard a racket outside. They rushed out, and to their shock, they saw their father Thomas sitting atop a large wagon. His brother-in-law had offered to drive his rig as a means of moving Thomas, his new wife **Sarah Bush Johnston Lincoln** and their belongings from Kentucky to Pigeon Creek, Indiana.

Whatever anger Abraham and his sister harbored for their father for having deserted them so soon after the death of their mother dissolved in the disbelief they experienced when helping unload their stepmother's belongings. She had an expensive bureau, a table with chairs, a large clothes chest, cooking utensils, knives, forks, and bedding. It was more household goods than the Lincoln children had ever seen. And their stepmother had brought them a new stepbrother, John, and two new step-sisters, Matilda and Sarah.

Thomas Lincoln had led his new wife to believe that he had a fine homestead in good condition. She was shocked when she saw the truth of their circumstances. The cabin was filthy and in need of many repairs. The Lincoln children were in a worse state than the cabin. Sarah decided that she had made a rough bargain, but would hug it all the tighter. She scrubbed the cabin clean, and the Lincoln children along with it. Their appearance had become shockingly bad during the absence of their father. Tattered clothing hung from their shoulders, loosely attached by very few threads; they were gaunt from lack of proper meals, wore no shoes and washed irregularly at best. Within days, Sarah's ministrations did wonders. She would later say I "...made them look a little more human. "[14] Both children felt like a great dark cloud that had settled over their cabin for months had been lifted.

Sarah Bush Lincoln, like Nancy before her, argued with her husband over the need for the children to attend school. Thomas reluctantly agreed to let them do so. He knew that Abraham was growing quickly, and could soon be a source of extra income for the family. It was tradition in 19th century frontier communities that children, when big enough, be hired out to neighbors to perform any number of odd jobs. The children's wages went directly to their parents. With their parents in agreement on the matter, Abraham and his sister Sarah began attending a school four miles from their cabin, run by Andrew Crawford. Abraham would attend this school on and off, with many interruptions for work contracted for him by his father, until he was fourteen years old.

***

With a large family of step-brothers and sisters, Dennis Hanks, and his own sister Sarah, Abraham began to live the life of a typical frontier youth. There was always work to be done. Once the farm chores were completed, Thomas would begin woodworking projects, building simple furniture for paying customers. He continually tried to involve Abe in this work, hoping to make his son as proficient as he was at the craft, but Abe showed little interest. His ambitions were already loftier than accepting the life his father enjoyed. This created constant ill-feeling between them. Abraham preferred to be hired out to neighbors, and spent months at a time working at neighboring farms, far from his father's constant criticism. He was popular as a hired hand, especially with the neighbor ladies. As Ward Hill Lamon observed in his biography of Lincoln, Abe was always ready to help them "...make fire, carry water, or nurse a baby,"[15] in addition to the work he was hired to perform.

Thomas was angry with Abe's preoccupation with reading and writing. He believed that these "lazy" habits could make Abe less marketable to neighbors looking for a hardworking hired hand, and therefore limit the family's income. Nearby farmers, impressed by Abe's size and strength, overlooked his strange fascination with book learning and hired him anyway.

Social activities occasionally interrupted the seemingly endless work routine of the families in southern Indiana. The Lincolns and their neighbors would often attend a log rolling, house raising or wedding. Ward Hill Lamon describes the celebration at these events:

On such occasions the young women carried their shoes in their hands, and only put them on when about to join the company. The ladies drank whiskey-toddy, while the men took it straight; both sexes danced the live-long night, barefooted, on puncheon floors.[16]

Attending Sunday church was also welcome relief from day to day drudgery. Abraham and his siblings sometimes accompanied their parents, but usually they stayed at the cabin while Thomas and Sarah made their way to the **Pigeon Creek Church**. A neighbor, Mrs. Elizabeth Crawford, described the weekly ritual to Lincoln biographer William Herndon:

At that time we thought it nothing to go eight or ten miles. The old ladies did not stop for want of a shawl, or cloak, or riding dress...they would put on their husband's old overcoat, and wrap up their little ones and take one or two up on their beasts, and their husbands would walk and they would go to church and stay in the neighborhood until the next day, and then go home. They would come in laughing, shake hands all around, sit down and talk about their game they had killed or some other work they had done, and smoke their pipes together with the old ladies...Thus they spent the time till time for preaching to commence, then they would take their seats; the preacher would take his stand, draw his coat, open his shirt collar, commence service by singing and prayer; take his text and preach till the sweat would roll off in great drops. Shaking hands and singing then ended the service.[17]

***

When he was near 15 years old, Abraham began to display a taste for public speaking. When his parents went off to church he would gather up his brothers and sisters and conduct a mock service of his own. His step-sister, Matilda Johnston, later recalled what happened:

Abe would take down the Bible, read a verse, give out a hymn, and we would sing. He preached, and we would do all the crying. Sometimes he would join in the chorus of tears. One day my brother, John Johnston, caught a land terrapin, brought it to the place where Abe was preaching, threw it against the tree, and crushed the shell. It suffered much-quivered all over. Abe then preached against cruelty to animals, contending that an ant's life was as sweet to it as ours to us.[18]

Even when he was working a neighbor's fields as a hired hand, he would sometimes stop his laboring to mount a hay bale and begin speaking about some topic or another. Other hired help nearby would drop their tools and gather to listen to him, thus wasting good daylight work time, much to the dismay of the farmer who had hired them. "The sight of such a thing amused all", his step-mother Sarah said. All except his father Thomas, who, whenever he viewed such a scene, pulled Abe from off his platform, cuffed him and set him back to work.

Abraham continued his passion for reading. John Hanks, a cousin of Lincoln's mother Nancy, who came to live with the Lincoln's for four years in Indiana, described Abraham's habits:

When Abe and I returned to the house from work, he would go to the cupboard, snatch a piece of cornbread, take down a book(always borrowed from some neighbor near or far), sit down on a chair, cock his legs up high as his head, and read. He and I worked barefooted, grubbed it, ploughed, mowed, and cradled together; ploughed corn, gathered it, and shucked corn. Abraham read constantly when he had an opportunity.[19]

Some of the books he borrowed and read during these years include Aesop's Fables, Robinson Crusoe, A Pilgrim's Progress, and Parson Weems Life of Washington. These adventures and fables transported him far away from his life in the Indiana woods, and began to broaden his awareness of a much larger world than he had yet seen.

When Abraham learned that a neighbor, Josiah Crawford, had purchased a new biography of George Washington, written by David Ramsey, he immediately walked several miles to Crawford's home and asked permission to take it home to read. Crawford, a mean-tempered and churlish man, reluctantly agreed to let Abraham do so. After Lincoln was done reading it one night, he carefully tucked it into a recess in the cabin wall. A storm blew through the area, and when Lincoln retrieved the book the next day to continue his reading, he discovered it had been badly damaged by rain that had soaked it during the storm. When he tried to return it to Mr. Crawford, the old man refused it, saying Lincoln needed to pay him for it, or work off the debt in his fields. Abraham had no money to pay Crawford, so he pulled fodder for four days at 25 cents a day to cover the debt.

One book in particular, Aesop's Fables, which friends said Lincoln almost always carried with him, along with a copy of the Bible, held passages that foreshadowed who he would become.

An Aesop fable called The Old Man and His Sons contained the following thought: "A kingdom divided against itself is brought to desolation."[20] Lincoln echoed this exact theme in some of his greatest speeches later in life.

Another entitled The Unstrung Bow ends with the following moral: "If you keep a bow always bent, it will break presently; but if you let it go back, it will be fitter for use when you want it...Sports and diversions soothe and slaken it (the mind) and keep it in condition to be exerted to the best advantage upon occasion."[21] It is a little recorded fact that Lincoln, in his adult life, enjoyed participating in many of the sports popular in his day, such a fives (a form of street bowling), wrestling and handball. He was admired by his neighbors in New Salem and Springfield for his strength and agility.

In the fable The Ape and the Fox it is stated: "A weak man should not aspire to be a king. To be qualified for such an office, an office of the last importance to mankind, the person should be of a distinguished, prudent, and of most unblemished integrity, too honest to impose upon others, and too penetrating to be imposed upon." [22]

The man we all know now as "Honest Abe" read these words at age 15, and went on quoting from Aesop's Fables for years.

***

One of the most pleasant tasks a boy had to learn on the frontier was hauling corn to the local grist mill to be ground into cornmeal. As soon as a boy was big enough to mount a horse and handle heavy bags of corn, he would ride with his father or some older children to the chosen mill, learning the proper paths to travel, and what to do to process their corn when they arrived there. Eventually he would be expected to do so without any adult supervision. It was a pleasant task because it gave a young boy the chance to meet new people, see new places, hear new stories, and practice telling some of his own.

Lincoln made this journey many times to Huffman's Mill on Anderson Creek, sixteen miles from his cabin. Eventually Gordon's Mill was built, only two miles from the Lincoln cabin. It was the site of Lincoln's next brush with death.

Sometime around 1821 (the exact date is not known), Lincoln was at the mill waiting in line to get his corn ground. A farmer's horse was tethered to a beam that connected to a large stone wheel that ground the produce to a coarse powdered corn meal. As the horse lazily walked in a circle, turning the large stone wheel, Abraham commented that, "...his dog could eat the meal as fast as the mill could grind it." Finally, his turn came and Abraham hitched his horse to the beam. It began its slow march around the circle. As Carl Sandburg records in his Prairie Years, Volume One, Abraham urged the animal on saying "Git up, you old hussy, git up...", while striking it lightly with a switch to keep it moving. Suddenly, the horse reared and loosed a strong kick to Lincoln's head, knocking him unconscious. His head was bandaged and he was taken home, and put to bed, unconscious. He woke 24 hours later and spoke his first words, "...you old hussy," finishing the sentence he had been speaking to his horse when it kicked him the day before.[22]

Once again death had flitted close by Abraham Lincoln. Some historians believe that as a result of this accident, he developed a "lazy eye," with his left eye occasionally drifting off center focus, especially in times of stress.

***

By 1824, Abraham Lincoln was 15 years old, and had nearly reached his full adult height of six feet four inches. Two acquaintances of his described him at this age. Anna Gentry, a classmate of Abraham's, related her memories of him in an interview for William Herndon, done late in her life:

Abe was an honest boy—a good boy—all liked him—was friendly—somewhat sociable-not so much so as we wanted him-Abe was a long-thin-leggy-gawky boy dried up and shriveled.[23]

Anna's observations may explain Lincoln's shyness and lack of success with girls at this stage of his life.

In an interview with the authors of A History of Warrick, Spencer and Perry Counties, Indiana, a worker at one of the grist mills that Lincoln frequented in Indiana remembered him:

...a tall, beardless boy about my own age dressed in a suit of well-worn brown jeans, the trousers of which he had long before outgrown, and wearing a woolen hat and coarse, heavy, plain-cut leather shoes of the style then in vogue among the backwoods people, came riding up to the mill.[24]

In this same year, 1824, Abraham Lincoln was witness to an event that haunted him for years to come. Matthew Gentry was a classmate of Abraham's, and three years his senior. He was a bright young man, who was the son of one of the richest men in a poor region, and as such, he was highly regarded by his teachers and fellow students. One day at home, without warning, Matthew began to shout hysterically, attempted to maim himself, fought violently with his father and attacked his mother. Lincoln, who was there that day visiting the family, was shocked by the unexpected breakdown of his friend. He travelled to the Gentry home on several occasions after the incident, and watched as his friend Matthew sat on the floor rocking back and forth, moaning and wailing like a wolf in the night woods. It seemed inexplicable to Lincoln how this fortune favored young man could become completely unhinged. Lincoln brooded over it for years, trying to reason out the purpose of such a cruel turn of fate.

In 1826 Abraham's sister, Sarah, married a neighbor, Aaron Grigsby. Her marriage was not a happy one. Word reached the Lincolns that Aaron was treating Sarah badly, and a family feud started. The two families agreed to settle the feud in the pioneer fashion, with a fist fight. Abraham was to fight Aaron's brother William, but William refused, claiming that Lincoln was too big for him to make it a fair battle. The Lincolns then settled on Abraham's step-brother John Johnston to fight for Sarah's honor. The fight went on for some time, and was eventually declared a draw. One bystander, who tried to enter the fight to aid William Grigsby, got his shoulder dislocated by

Abraham, who stopped him from interfering.

Sarah's marriage was not only unhappy, but short. Two years after becoming man and wife, Sarah Lincoln, age nineteen, died in childbirth. The manner of her death caused further dislike of the Grigsbys by the Lincolns. A neighbor recalled what happened the day Sarah died. "My mother was there at the time. She had a strong voice, and I heard her calling father...He went after a doctor, but it was too late. They let her lay too long."[25]

Abraham was at a Grigsby relative's house when he was told the news. One of the family present at the time said that he "...sat down in the door of the smoke house and buried his face in his hands. The tears slowly trickled between his bony fingers and his gaunt frame shook with sobs. We turned away."[26]

According to friends, Abraham felt that Sarah's death came as a result of the Grigsby's neglect of her.

Lincoln struggled to fit the events of his own life into some framework that would explain life in general. By age 19 he had already seen his baby brother, aunt, uncle, mother and sister die, and had come close to death himself twice already. He must have questioned whether there was some larger purpose for it all, seen only by a power greater than man, or whether all humanity was alone in facing the random nature of events. And, if there was a greater power, why was all this death being visited on him? He recalled his mother Nancy's Bible stories about how God tested hard-working, God-fearing Job. Was he being tested? Was there some unseen purpose for which he was being prepared?

William Kolasinski

Chapter Three

RIVER MAN

A braham spent the next several months toiling in the fields of neighbors, interrupted frequently by harangues from his father for reading too much and working too little, and by visits to Gordon's grist mill to swap stories and grind corn. Then, one day in late 1828, while he was in Gentryville, he received a job offer that would change his life. James Gentry, the owner of the town's grocery, was sending a flatboat full of his goods down to New Orleans. He needed someone to help his son Allen build the boat and guide it safely to its destination. Allen had made the trip once before with his father, but James Gentry knew how dangerous it could be, and he believed that Lincoln's size, strength and reputation for honesty made him the perfect companion for his son on the journey.

In October, Lincoln and Allen Gentry headed to Rockport, Indiana, a small town of 100 inhabitants, located on the banks of the Ohio River, and began construction of **the flatboat.** They

41

completed the boat in early December, in time to begin the loading of goods. Harvests had concluded and the produce was ready for shipment. It is not known exactly what they carried onboard, but farmers of the time typically shipped bushels of corn and oats, barrels of pork, corn meal and beans, bacon hams and venison hams. Lincoln and Gentry's boat probably contained some combination of those goods.

Abraham and Allen set off on their trip on December 18th, 1828. The two men would travel 1,200 miles downriver from Rockport, Indiana to New Orleans, navigating the constantly changing channels of the Ohio and Mississippi rivers. They would need to remain vigilant at all times. There were hidden sandbars that could leave them aground, large tree branches jutting out of the river bottom that could rip into the side of their craft, and thieves who might try to board the vessel while it lay tied up along the riverbank at night.

The trip, while fraught with dangers, also held exciting opportunities for the young men; they would hear people speaking with strange accents, see ships larger than any they had ever seen and visit cities with thousands of inhabitants. They would not come back from this journey the same men they were when they left.

***

Once Abraham steered the flatboat out into the middle of the Ohio River, they were borne along at speeds of 4-6 miles per hours, heading west toward the confluence of the Ohio and Mississippi rivers. When they entered into the Illinois area they passed a notorious landmark at **Cave-in-the Rock.** For years this large cave on the Illinois shore sported a sign that was clearly visible to passing flatboats. It read Wilson's Liquor Vault and House of Entertainment. Many tired and thirsty flatboat crews had polled their boats ashore here to drink in the pleasures that Wilson's establishment had to offer. They got far more than they bargained for. Once a crew had drunk themselves nearly senseless, they were lured up to the second floor (the cave was so spacious that it actually had two stories of rooms built inside it) with promises of more liquor and women. There they would be set upon by the Wilson gang and murdered. The gang would empty the dead men's pockets, then, find the unfortunate crew's flatboat, and steal all of its cargo. When they were done they would sink the boat and dispose of the bodies. Authorities eventually found over 60 bodies hidden in the cave. Fortunately for Lincoln and Gentry, by the time they came upon it, the cave had been abandoned and the gang arrested.

Abraham and Allen did not record a daily diary of their events. Fortunately, an Englishman and Member of Parliament named Colonel John Baille, did. He departed on a similar journey just weeks before Lincoln and Gentry. We can experience what Gentry and Lincoln did through Baille's notes.

When he reached Louisville, Kentucky, Baille wrote:

The number of steamboats here is almost incredible. I understand there were upwards of 500 on the Mississippi and Ohio alone...Went on board several that were lying below us. The largest, called the Washington is built like a three storied house, with every accommodation that could be found in a good hotel.[1]

As the journey continued, the scenery became repetitive.

...during the whole day we had no view save the interminable forest, and dull ragged banks on both sides. Subject as this part of the country is to yearly inundation, very few settlements have yet been attempted, and these generally on high bluffs...We passed only one today, where I observed something like the appearance of a village.[2]

Lincoln and Gentry fried cornmeal cakes and pork for meals, and sometimes enjoyed a wild turkey dinner after Gentry shot one of the many birds seen daily in the area of the rivers. They washed their clothes, and hung them out to dry on ropes strung from the cabin to the rudder post.

After weeks of river travel through nearly uninhabited lands, Lincoln and Gentry reached Natchez, Louisiana. This town of 5,000 people, the largest Lincoln had seen up to that day, was a bustling trade center where flatboats usually stopped to begin trading some of their produce for cash or other manufactured goods. The two young men undoubtedly traded or sold some of their goods here.

The Englishman John Baille recorded his impression of the area:

...the forests are now covered everywhere with Spanish Moss, which attached itself to the trees, but typically to the Cypress...you see it hanging from all parts of the trees in dark and somber festoons, adding a funereal aspect to the dark and dreary view; quite in character however, with the deadly malignity of the climate.[3]

Lincoln and Gentry enjoyed an uneventful trip down the Mississippi River up to this point. Most daytime hours found Lincoln working the sweeps and rudder, steering the boat, with Gentry cleaning up the cabin, preparing their simple meals, and, as they offloaded their goods in trades with passing towns, moving the cargo about on the deck, in order to avoid foundering due to uneven weight distribution.

Trouble came when they reached the "Sugar Coast" area of the Mississippi River below Natchez. Huge fields of cotton and sugar cane lined the banks of the river in this region, worked during the day by hundreds of slaves. Lincoln and Gentry tied their boat up for the night somewhere along the banks of a plantation owned by a "Mrs. Duquesne," and lay down for hard earned sleep. A group of seven Negroes had seen them tying up their boat, and saw that it was manned by only two young men. They hatched a plan to enter the boat late at night, murder the crew, unload its cargo for sale later, and sink the flatboat to hide their crime. Hours after the two man crew fell asleep, the Negro gang climbed aboard the boat. The noise awakened Lincoln and Gentry. Lincoln came at the men with a large crab tree club he had fashioned for self-defense. Gentry, thinking quickly as he saw Lincoln attempting to handle more men than they both could, called to Lincoln, "get the guns and let's shoot!" Hearing that the men had guns, the Negroes fled quickly. Gentry was unharmed, but Lincoln had taken a solid blow to the head, causing a wound that would leave a scar above either his right eye or ear, depending which story you chose to believe.

Another close brush with death for Lincoln, still only 19 years of age.

After passing a restless remainder of the night, the two men set off downriver to complete the first part of their journey. When they docked in New Orleans, it must have seemed like the whole sky was blotted out by the masts of the ships moored there. A local newspaper, the New Orleans Price Current and Commercial Intelligencer, noted that on one typical day in 1828, the docks of New Orleans held 66 ships, 85 brigs, 30 schooners, 6 sloops and 20 steamboats, from such foreign ports as Hamburg and Bremen Germany, Gibraltar Spain, Aberdeen Scotland, Havana Cuba, and Vera Cruz Mexico, along with ships from the American cities of Philadelphia, New York, Baltimore, Providence and Pensacola. The backwoods boys from Indiana must have been awestruck.

The two young men set off to locate buyers for the goods on their flatboat. Once they did so, only two other things remained to be done; see the city and book passage on a steamer homebound for Indiana. They would not linger long in New Orleans, for Allen Gentry was anxious to be with his wife and new son.

The allure of the city must have been powerful for these two young men who had yet seen so little of life. The streets they walked were brightly festooned with the flags of France, England and the United States. They watched Russian sailors, drinking and singing loudly in a language they could not understand. They saw Swedes, Norwegians and Englishmen flirting in sidewalk cafes with gaudily dressed ladies who seemed to invite their attentions with a flash of their painted eyes. They stared as a group of octoroons and quadroons strolled by, struck by the beauty of their luxuriant skin, radiating colors from creamed coffee to mahogany. Everywhere they went, as Carl Sandburg described, they heard the locals talking of "niggers, good and bad niggers, how to rawhide the bad ones with mule whips or bring 'em to N'Orleans and sell 'em; and how you could trust your own children with a good nigger."[4]

Allen Gentry later recalled, "We stood and watched the slaves sold in New Orleans, and Abraham was very angry. " Gentry claimed that Lincoln said, "If I ever get the chance to hit this thing, I'll hit it hard."[5]

Lincoln and Gentry booked return passage on a steamer, Lincoln's first such trip, and came home to Indiana. When he received his pay, over $16 dollars, Abraham was richer than he had ever been in his life, but not for long. He turned it all over to his father, as was the custom.

In the months after his return from New Orleans, Abraham's life returned to its monotonous routine. When work on his family land was finished, Abraham was hired out by his father to work on neighboring farms. His taste of freedom on the river must have gnawed at him during the long hours and days of toil in the fields.

***

March 1829 found twenty-year-old Abraham Lincoln helping his father put in crops on their farm. But even as he turned the soil and dropped the seeds for the new growing season, Lincoln was thinking ahead, to when he turned 21, and could begin to live his own life. He had asked a neighbor, William Wood, to inquire of the businesses along the Ohio River in Rockport, whether they needed a hired hand to assist them.

Nathaniel Grigsby, for whom Lincoln pulled fodder that year, described him at the time:

His breeches & socks didn't meet by 12 inches-Shin bones sharp-blue and narrow. Lincoln said to me one day that his father taught him to work but never learned him to love it.[6]

***

Lincoln was beginning to sort out his thoughts about politics and the current events often discussed around the area. He made the acquaintance of William Jones while working for a time at the Gentry Store in Rockport, Indiana. Jones was a clerk there, and Lincoln was doing odd jobs for the store owner. Jones allowed Abraham to read the newspapers that the store sold, and this provided Lincoln with hard information to help him shape his political philosophy.

His earliest political knowledge had come from listening to his father talk with the family about the virtues of **Senator Henry Clay** of Kentucky. Clay was a leading member of the Whig Party, whose national platform called for internal improvements (which promised better roads and means of transporting farm goods to market), high protective tariffs (to drive up the cost of imported goods and thereby allow American small business to compete with their larger, more efficient European counterparts), and a national bank (which would assure sound money and accessibility to loans). These positions had great appeal to the frontier farming class into which Lincoln's family fit. Also, Thomas Lincoln's uncle came from Lexington, Kentucky, Henry Clay's hometown.

A relative, John Hanks, stated: "I can say that Abe was never a Democrat, he was always a Whig; so was his father before him."

Sarah Bush Lincoln, Abraham's step-mother, had several close relations who held local elective offices. Politics was always discussed at the Lincoln dinner table. Sarah once told her step-son that he "ought to go into politics, because when he got to argyin,' the other feller'd purty soon say he had enough."[7]

The Gentry store where Abraham sometimes worked served four townships, with one named Jackson (after Democratic President Andrew Jackson) and another named Clay (after Whig leader Henry Clay). The political leanings of these townships mirrored their namesakes, so Lincoln certainly overheard many heated discussions by store patrons about their political heroes. He worked on his public speaking style and shaped his political opinions while joining in these cracker barrel debates.

When his work day was completed, Lincoln liked to attend the local court in Rockport. Unlike today, trials then were like local public theatre. Many people in surrounding communities attended court sessions, cheering on their favorite lawyers. Lincoln was particularly fascinated with the lawyer's command of law and language, and watching them increased his already strong desire to improve himself.

Two lawyers in particular drew his attention. John A. Brackenridge and John Pitcher both frequently argued cases in the courts at Rockport, and Lincoln was there as often as he could to see them. Local tradition had Brackenridge hosting Lincoln at his home, and even loaning the inquisitive youth some of his law books to read.

John Pitcher was only fourteen years older than Lincoln, but had already made a name for himself in the region as a talented and ambitious lawyer. A local journal, A History of Warrick, Spencer and Perry Counties, contains the following sketch of the man:

He was a practitioner of marked ability ... a hard student, deep in law, extremely accurate in his judgement... The character of his address to the court or jury was always dignified and at times brilliant and eloquent. He was extremely forcible, as quick as powder to grasp a point.[8]

In an interview with Jesse Weik, (who together with William Herndon wrote a great biography of Lincoln), Pitcher said, "I understood he (Lincoln) wanted to become a lawyer and I tried to encourage him." To a different source he also said of young Lincoln, that "He was nothing but a long, lean, gawky country jake. In fact, I did not think he had it in him."[9]

Pitcher may have had conflicting opinions about Lincoln at the time, but he did help him. Late in his life he showed a visitor to his home a two-volume set of Blackstone's Commentaries (essential reading for any would be lawyer), "in which, on the flyleaf (of one)was inscribed the name A. Lincoln."[10]

There is no definitive evidence, beyond Picher's claims, that Lincoln at age twenty had yet made up his mind to become a lawyer. His experiences with Allen Gentry on the flatboat journey to New Orleans were fresh in his mind, and were, to date, the most exciting ones of his young life.

William Kolasinski

Chapter Four

COMING OF AGE

On February 12, 1830, Abraham Lincoln turned twenty-one years of age. This was a milestone of great importance in a young man's life. It meant he was independent, in the legal sense. His father could no longer hire him out and expect to receive the son's wages from that work.

Lincoln had been considering his future after this birthday. He had determined that whatever course he chose to pursue, he would make sure his parents were safe and secure. Starting that fall he had begun to help his father build a new cabin to replace their old one. William Wood, a neighbor, recalled:

I saw him cutting down a large tree one day; I asked him what he was going to do with it; he said he was going to saw it into planks for his father's new house...Abe cut the tree down and he ...whipsawed it into planks.[1]

Even as the new Lincoln cabin began to take shape in the Pigeon Creek settlement, winds of change began to alter the family's future. They began to receive letters from John Hanks, a relative of Abraham's mother, Nancy. Hanks had moved a year or so before from Pigeon Creek, Indiana to Macon County in Illinois, to see firsthand about rumors of fertile farmland there, available at low cost. Thomas Lincoln had been skeptical of these rumors, but he encouraged Hanks to find out the truth about them. John Hanks letters spoke of farmland so fertile that all one needed to do to plant a crop was to turn the soil and drop seeds. Anything could and would grow there. Hanks urged the family to leave the rock strewn, weed choked lands of Indiana and come to Illinois and settle there.

Thomas Lincoln was not about to leave the farmland he and his family had worked so hard to carve out of the wilderness. They were growing more crops than they could consume, and selling the excess for profit. They had friends, membership in the community church, and the respect of their neighbors. Dennis Hanks, the adopted son of William and Betsy Hanks (who had died in the same milk-sick outbreak that killed Abraham's mother Nancy) was living with the Lincolns at the time at Pigeon Creek. He was excited by the picture John Hanks painted, of a prosperous future in Illinois, and decided to travel to Illinois to see for himself if the opportunities there were as bright as John Hanks claimed they were. He returned convinced that Illinois was where he needed to be. He then convinced his stepbrother, Squire Hall, to join him in the move. This created a great turmoil in the Lincoln family, for Dennis and Squire were married to Elizabeth and Matilda Johnston, daughters of Thomas Lincoln's wife, Sarah. She began to implore her husband to join in the move to Illinois, for she "...could not think of parting with them." When another outbreak of the milk-sick disease was reported in the region, Thomas decided there were enough good reasons to pull up stakes, so he told his wife to start packing, for they were heading to Illinois.

Abraham was surprised by the decision, but being a good son, he decided to remain for a while more with his family and assist them with their move. His future, whether it be flat-boating, the law, or something else, would have to wait.

Weeks were taken up in preparation to leave. Thomas and Sarah journeyed to Elizabethtown, Kentucky, and sold the town lot and cabin she had lived in with her late husband prior to marrying Thomas Lincoln. She received $123 for the sale, an excellent profit considering she had purchased the lot twelve years before for just $25.

A week before their scheduled departure date for Illinois, they sold their 100 acres of land in Indiana, along with 100 hogs, and four to five hundred bushels of corn. They would be leaving Indiana with over $500 cash in hand, a very respectable sum for the time.

Dennis Hanks, Squire Hall, Abraham and Thomas Lincoln set about building three crude wagons, one for each family. A neighbor described the vehicles:

There was not a nail or piece of iron in it. The whole structure was fastened together with wooden pins and the tires were made of (covered in) rawhide.[2]

$100 of the money gained in the property and land sales was used to purchase two pairs of oxen, and one pair of horses to be used to pull the heavily loaded conveyances.

Finally, on the first of May, 1830, the party was ready to depart. Shouts of "Good Luck!" rang out from the crowd of neighbors who had come to see them off. The shouts were nearly drowned out by the noise the wagons made. One of the people seeing them off, Raymond Grigsby, said that the wagons "were very musical, for the more grease one put on the wooden axle to make it run lightly the more it would squeak and squeal, making a noise that could be heard for a mile."

It was not "the Lincoln party" that set out that day for Illinois, for Thomas, Sarah and Abraham were only one of the families headed to Illinois. Dennis and Elizabeth Hanks and their four children, Squire and Matilda Hall and their son, were in the caravan as well. As they headed four miles north to travel the Troy-Vincennes Trace that would take them to the Indiana state line, Abraham must have thought of those left behind, buried on a small tree-shaded knoll near their cabin at Pigeon Creek; his mother, Nancy, his sister Sarah, and his aunt and uncle.

***

Just before crossing the Kaskaskia River into Illinois, the wagon train of Lincoln kin stopped for a day's rest in Vincennes, Indiana. There, according to A.H.H. Chapman (husband of Abraham's step-sister Elizabeth), Lincoln saw his first printing press. Books were still a rare thing on the frontier, and printing presses like the one Lincoln saw were rarer still. He was fascinated by its mechanisms, and spent some time questioning Elihu Stout, the gentleman who owned it, and used it to produce the Vincennes Western Sun newspaper.

The party crossed the river the next day and began to move through a vast, open prairie. The yellow and red clay of southern Indiana gave way to the rich black loam of Macon County, Illinois. Grasses grew to over six feet tall, hiding from sight any people or animals that passed through them. Their roots were numerous and thick, and it would take a strong man wielding a heavy axe to drive a wooden stake into the ground they covered.

The members of the little wagon train met settlers who spoke of how tough it was to clear a field, how plow blades would break battling to split the tough sod. They also spoke of the great crop yields that could be expected once they did get their crops planted, and of how farm animals would grow lean through the rough winters, but would fatten and get gleaming coats when they grazed on the luxuriant spring grasses. As the caravan wound its way further into the state, they saw wild horses and hogs roaming the fields. They must have thought John Hanks to be completely truthful in his praise of the place.

After fifteen days of travel the wagon train reached Decatur, Illinois, a small trading center and county seat, in central Illinois. They inquired of a townsman where they might find the cabin of John Hanks, and upon learning that he lived some four miles away, continued their journey until they found his place. John was thrilled to see that his relatives had made the trip without incident. He told them that he had a good spot picked out for them some six miles south, and that he would take them there the following day. After a pleasant night spent reconnecting, the party set off in the early morning and made the trek to a small clearing on a bluff located on the north bank of a branch of the Sangamon River. Thomas was pleased to see that John Hanks had already chopped down several trees, which lay piled up and ready for use in building a new cabin.

Thomas Lincoln began to turn the sod, working had to tear through the thick grasses that grew on his land. Eventually he cleared fifteen acres, ready for planting. While he did this, Abraham and John Hanks split out the rails to fence in the area.

In mid-June Abraham and some members of his family, attended the wedding of Mary (Polly) Warnick to Joseph Stevens, at her father's farm three miles away. Polly was daughter of Major William Warnick, a prominent and prosperous neighbor. Soon after making Abraham's acquaintance, Major Warnick hired him to split 1,000 rails by the end of winter.[3]

During one of his visits to Decatur with Dennis Hanks, the two heard candidates for the State Legislature speaking at a campaign gathering. Not liking what they heard from the candidates, Dennis Hanks urged Lincoln to reply to them. Lincoln mounted a hay bale and made his first political speech. It was a brief, well-reasoned and well received call for improvement of the Sangamon River, to allow for boats carrying produce from local farms to more easily navigate it.[4]

No longer bound to turn his earnings over to his father, Abraham continued to

accept jobs where and when he could find them. He split four hundred rails for a nearby farmer, and used his pay to buy cloth that he had made into a pair of brown jean trousers, the first new pair he ever owned. Fall came, and with it, chills, fever and ague. His father and step-sister fell ill. They fought off the sickness by consuming doses of "Barks," a Peruvian bark and whiskey tonic mixture that they bought at Renshaw's General Store in Decatur.

During Christmas week, 1831, the snow began to fall. It continued for two days straight, piling up two and a half feet of snow. The temperatures dropped to twenty below zero, and winds whipped at blizzard speeds. Then a short period of warmth came, and with it, rain. As the rain fell on the piles of snow, it began forming a thick crust of ice everywhere. Then temperatures dropped again, and more snow began to fall. Soon depths of drifts on the prairie reached four and a half feet. Cows, hogs and horses died in the fields, as did many of their owners who tried to brave the weather to save them. Families, unable to go outside, ran out of wood for fires. Some died in their cabins from the cold. Others died from starvation, unable to gather in their corn supplies buried nearby beneath the snowdrifts. Locals who survived this winter referred to it in years to come as "the winter of the Big Snow," and proudly called themselves "Snowbirds."

Lincoln, believing a bargain made was a bargain to be kept, left the safety of his cabin in February after the snows let up, and trekked three miles through the deep drifts to the farm of Major Warnick, intent on **finishing his job of splitting 1,000 rails** for the man. As he crossed the frozen Sangamon River, his feet broke through the ice, and became severely frostbitten. Mrs. Warnick put snow on his feet to take out the frostbite, then rubbed them with grease made of "rabbit bile."[60] Lincoln finished the job for Major Warnick and return to his family's cabin, where he remained for the balance of the winter, recuperating.

***

With the onset of spring, Lincoln, along with step-brother John D. Johnston and John Hanks, built a flatboat at Sangamo Town. Who they built it for is not known. When that job was completed, they returned to John Hank's cabin, near the Decatur area, where they met a true frontier character named **Denton Offutt**, who would play a key role in the next years of Lincoln's life.

Carl Sandburg described Offutt as "...a hard drinker, a hustler, and a talker, shrewd with his tongue, easy with promises, a believer in pots of gold at the rainbow's end." Mentor Graham, a school teacher living in New Salem and soon to be a tutor to Abraham Lincoln in his constant search for knowledge and improvement, thought Offutt to be "an unsteady – noisy – fussy – rattle brained man, wild and unprovidential." Hardin Bale, another citizen of New Salem, and future neighbor of Lincoln's, believed Offutt to be "...a gassy – windy – brain rattling man."[5]

Offutt asked Lincoln, Johnston and Hanks to meet him near Springfield, at a village on the Sangamon River, "...as soon as the snow got off." If they did so, he promised them that he would have a flatboat loaded with produce there, ready for them to pilot down to New Orleans. Their pay would be twelve dollars a month. Offutt may have struck many people as strange and untrustworthy, but Lincoln, Johnston and Hanks saw in him a good payday, doing work they knew and would enjoy. In early March, 1831 the three men travelled to the agreed upon rendezvous point, but could not find Offutt anywhere. Some locals told them that they thought Offutt was in Springfield, a small village just down river, so the trio headed there. They found Offutt in a place called the Buckhorn Tavern, drunk and semi-conscious. After a good sobering-up, Offutt confessed that he had not yet secured a flatboat or gathered his stores to load onto the boat. He promised to remain sober for the remainder of their time together, and with that assurance, final plans were made. Lincoln, Johnston and Hanks departed to gather the tools and supplies necessary, and build the flatboat. Offutt was to gather up his stores and ready them for loading once the boat was done.

In late March, Erastus Wright, Assessor of Sangamon County, saw Lincoln in Sangamo Town, working on the flatboat, "boots off, hat, coat and vest off. Pants rolled up to his knees and shirt wet with sweat, and combing his fuzzy hair with his fingers as he pounded away on the boat."[6]

By April 18th, the flatboat was completed. John Johnston, John Hanks, Abraham Lincoln and Denton Offutt loaded goods on board and began polling into the current of the Sangamon River, headed to New Orleans.

They did not get far. The next day, while rounding a curve of the river at the village of New Salem, **the flatboat hung up on the dam of the Rutledge/Cameron mill.** The bow of the boat was driven onto the edge of the dam, raising it up, with the stern sunk into the water behind it. Barrels of pork began sliding astern, causing the boat to take on water even faster. Townspeople began gathering at the shoreline to see if and how the flatboat would get freed from its lodgment.

They saw a tall young man finally take command of the situation, dressed in a "...pair of blue jean trousers indefinitely rolled up, a cotton shirt, striped white and blue,...and a buckeye-chip hat for which a demand of twelve and a half cents would be exorbitant."[7] He directed his crewmates to move the barrels at the stern of the boat off, and onto another boat anchored nearby. As the barrels were moved, the weight distribution onboard shifted from the stern to the center of the craft, so that it was now floating evenly, balanced on the dam like a teeter-totter. Lincoln then climbed off the flatboat, waded ashore, walked uphill into the town, and borrowed an auger from Onstott's cooper shop. With the auger, he returned to his boat and bored a hole through the deck and bottom of the bow, and the water drained from the flatboat. With the water drained, and the load lightened, the four crewmen were able to ease the flatboat over the dam. Once free, they steered the flatboat to shore and hopped onto land, to the applause of the citizens of New Salem gathered there. The townspeople marveled at the ingenuity of the tall young fellow, whose name they learned, was Abraham Lincoln. He didn't look like much, but his cleverness definitely left an impression with them.

The crew spent the rest of the day reloading and securing the barrels they had moved. Then they headed up the hill into town, where the townspeople treated them to food and drink and lodging for the night. Denton Offutt, always on the lookout for opportunities, took note of the friendliness of the crowd, and the location of New Salem on the banks of a navigable river. He decided that this place had the potential to become a trading center. He just might build a store here when he came back from New Orleans.

Early the next morning, Offutt, Lincoln, Johnston and Hanks boarded their flatboat and departed New Salem, bound for New Orleans. The trip was uneventful. In Saint Louis, Missouri, John Hanks left the boat, feeling that the most difficult part of the journey was over, and that his family needed him to help get their crops planted. He returned to central Illinois, while Lincoln, Johnston and Offutt completed the trip to New Orleans at the "high" speed of four to six miles per hour, depending on the prevailing winds and currents. They reached New Orleans in May. They were all speechless as they gazed at the unbelievable number of craft moored at this busy port. They anchored their vessel as close to the shore as they could and then walked almost a mile, climbing from one boat deck to another, until they finally reached shore. They made their way carefully through the wharves, packed tight with piles of cotton bales, barrels of pork, and sacks of flour. The din from flatboat crew's laughter, fights, and drinking bouts rang in their ears. They also heard the cries and curses of shippers who had just realized that they would head home broke, their cargo unsellable because it had spoiled while on the long journey to New Orleans.

In town, Lincoln saw once again the painful reality of the slave trade. A newspaper carried an advertisement:

We have now on hand, and intend to keep throughout the entire year, a large and well-selected stock of Negroes, consisting of field hands, house servants, mechanics, cooks, seamstresses, washers, ironers, etc., which we can sell and will sell as low or lower than any other house here or in New Orleans; persons wishing to purchase would do well to call on us before making purchases elsewhere, as our fresh and regular arrivals will keep us supplied with a good and general assortment; our terms are liberal; give us a call.[8]

Another seller advertised:

For sale - several likely girls from 10 to 18 years old, a woman 24, a very valuable woman 25, with three very likely children.[9]

At a square in the city they saw a live auction, where a young octoroon girl (a person who is one-eighth black by descent) was being offered for sale to the gathered crowd of mostly male buyers. The girl was made to show her teeth to prove they were sound, lift her skirts so that buyers could examine her legs to be sure of her ability to squat in the fields for long hours of labor, and to run back and forth, demonstrating that she was free of any lung condition.

These sights stayed with him, and in later years he spoke to friends of how shocked he was them.

***

While in New Orleans, Offutt spoke of the future, and of the little town of New Salem, Illinois. Offutt told Abraham that he was going to open a grocery there, and that he would like for Lincoln to run it for him. They came to an agreement, and Lincoln promised to meet him there in the summer to begin clerking at the store.

A month passed, with Lincoln and Johnston hiring out, loading coal onto steamships. They finally earned enough money to purchase tickets to travel to Saint Louis, Missouri. From there, they made their way by canoe, and then on foot, back to the Coles County area, where Lincoln stayed briefly with his mother and father. He explained to them that he was leaving, to work on his own in New Salem. The parting with his mother was sad and affectionate, each hugging the other. Sarah Bush Lincoln later said of her stepson:

I can say what scarcely one woman – a mother – can say in a thousand. Abe never gave me a cross word or look, and never refused, in fact or appearance, to do anything I requested him...He was dutiful to me always.[10]

His father shook his hand and bade him well, but later, as related by Carl Sandburg, Thomas Lincoln told a visitor:

I s'pose Abe is still fooling hisself with eddication. I tried to stop it, but he has got that fool idea in his head, and it can't be got out. Now, I hain't got no eddication, but I get along far better'n ef I had.[11]

Sandburg does not specifically cite his source for this comment, and it may be fictitious, but I believe it does capture the tone of the strained relationship between the two.

On July 8, 1831, in Springfield, Illinois, Denton Offutt paid $5 to obtain a license to retail merchandise in Sangamon County. This amount indicates that the stock he planned to begin his New Salem store with was valued at $1,000.

In late July, Abraham Lincoln returned to New Salem, Illinois, describing himself as "a floating piece of driftwood." For the first time in his life, he would be living alone, and on his own.

Chapter Five

IN SEARCH OF A FUTURE

New Salem was a small town, with big dreams. Twenty families called it home, the same number as inhabited the little village of Chicago up north. It sat on a tree-lined bluff, just above a curve in the Sangamon River. It's townspeople were hopeful that the Sangamon River would prove navigable for shallow draft ships, which would allow it to become a thriving trade center where nearby farmers could bring their corn crops, have them ground at the Rutledge/Cameron mill, packed into barrels, loaded onto boats

and shipped up and down river to be sold for profit.

Denton Offutt had not yet arrived in town, so Lincoln worked odd jobs to earn enough to pay for food and lodging at John Cameron's home. Here he began to meet all of his new neighbors, entertaining them with his story telling. One in particular, the lizard story, was repeated around the area for years to come. Lincoln told it as an event that had happened years before in Indiana. Benjamin Thomas, in his book "Lincoln's New Salem", retold it:

He (Lincoln) told of an old preacher who was accustomed to appear before his congregation dressed in a coarse linen shirt and old fashioned pantaloons with baggy legs and a flap in front, which buttoned tightly about his waist with a single button, thus making suspenders unnecessary. His shirt was also held together by a single button at the collar. Rising in his pulpit, he announced as his text: "I am the Christ, whom I shall represent today. " About that time a small lizard ran up inside his baggy trousers. Continuing his discourse, the preacher slapped at the lizard, but without success. As it continued to ascend, the old man loosened the button on his pantaloons and, with a swinging kick, divested himself of them. But the lizard was now above 'the equatorial line of waistband', exploring the small of his back. The sermon flowed steadily on, but in the midst of it the preacher tore open his collar button and with a sweep of his arm threw off the shirt. The congregation was dazed for an instant; but at length an old lady rose, stamped her foot, and shouted: "Well, if you represent Christ, I'm done with the Bible." [1]

It was this sort of irreverent humor that began to win him friends in New Salem.

Offutt, state issued grocery license in hand, finally showed up in town, and purchased a lot for $10. **There, he and Lincoln built a log cabin to house their store.**

Denton Offutt's store, New Salem, Ill. where Lincoln was employed as a clerk in 1831

They stocked it with salt, sugar, tea, coffee, molasses, butter and eggs, whiskey, tobacco, hardware, stoneware, cups and saucers, plates, dishes, calico prints, hats, bonnets, gloves, socks and shoes. Offutt hired **Billy Green**, son of the local judge Bowling Green, to help Lincoln identify which customers could be trusted to pay for their goods on credit.

Offutt never was one for subtlety. He was very proud of his new store clerk, and constantly bragged to the customers, "He (Lincoln) knows more than any man in the United States...Someday he will be President of the United States...He can outrun, out lift, outwrestle, and throw down any man in Sangamon County."[2]

Bill Clary, who ran a saloon just yards north of Offutt's store heard this boasting and bet Offutt $10 that Lincoln could not beat Jack Armstrong, the champion wrestler of the area, and leader of a gang of local roughs known as the Clary's Grove boys.

The match took place on a level patch of ground next to Offutt's store. Word spread quickly about the wrestling match, and a large crowd gathered, wagering everything from money to whiskey on whether the tall newcomer could best Jack Armstrong. Jack was shorter than Lincoln, but he was powerfully built with thick, muscular forearms and legs. The match began and Lincoln, with longer arms, was able for some time to keep Armstrong from wrapping him up in a powerful hold. Frustrated, Armstrong stamped his heel into Lincoln's right foot, clearly a foul under frontier rules. Lincoln lost his temper, grabbed Armstrong by the throat, lifted all 200 pounds of him off his feet and tossed him flat onto his back. Armstrong's gang, shocked to see their leader sprawled on the ground, then started to come at Lincoln, shouting that Lincoln had cheated. Armstrong pulled himself out of the dust, waved them off, and declared Lincoln the winner saying "He's the best feller that ever broke into this settlement."[3]

The match earned Lincoln the lifelong friendship of **Jack Armstrong** and his gang, and the respect of his rough and tumble frontier community. In the years to come Lincoln would spend many hours at the Armstrong cabin, being fussed over by Jack's wife Hannah, who was always trying to feed the rail thin Lincoln extra potions of her homemade bread with honey.

In early August an election was held for local offices, and Lincoln cast his first vote, on the porch of John Cameron's house. He was asked to help tally the votes, a sign that already he was considered by his neighbors to be trustworthy, and intelligent enough to be given such an important task.

Lincoln confided to **Mentor Graham**, the town school teacher, that he wanted to study grammar. Graham agreed that this would assist Lincoln greatly if he was serious about improving himself. He told Lincoln that a man named Vaner, who lived about six miles away, owned a copy of Kirkham's Grammar, and would probably be amenable to Lincoln's borrowing it to study. Graham had barely finished speaking when Lincoln bolted out the door. Hours later he returned, grinning and holding in his hand the book Graham had spoken of. He rarely was seen without it in the months that followed, working by candlelight with Mentor Graham to master English grammar.

New Salem was beginning to take on the trappings of an up and coming community. James Rutledge, owner of the inn and grist mill, announced that he was forming a debating and literary society, whose meetings would be held at his establishment. Any men in town who sought to improve themselves were urged to attend. Lincoln joined them. At each meeting, one member would take a turn, giving a speech about some current event or topic of general interest that they had researched. Then, the whole group would discuss and criticize the presentation.

When the night of Lincoln's presentation arrived, the members were eager to hear what this newcomer had to say. They knew he was an accomplished wrestler who had beaten Jack Armstrong, and they knew he could make them laugh. They all remembered the "lizard story." Everyone expected to be entertained.

Lincoln began haltingly, apologizing, and telling the crowd that he would do his best to squeeze out the ideas that were roiling around in his head. What followed was a well-reasoned, well-supported speech that surprised the audience with its seriousness and polish. Afterword, Lincoln heard that James Rutledge was going about town telling people that there "...was more than wit and fun" in Abraham Lincoln.

Knowing that James Rutledge thought well of him meant something to Abraham Lincoln. Rutledge was one of the leading men in the community, in whose establishment Lincoln had been living, on and off, for the past several months. Rutledge had a blonde-haired, blue-eyed, eighteen-year-old daughter named Anne, whose sweet disposition charmed everyone around her, including Abraham Lincoln.

Legal records make it clear how much the people of New Salem were coming to trust Lincoln, after only knowing him for five months. In late November he was asked by James Eastep to write a legal document, a bond for a deed. In December of 1831 he signed as a witness for three more such deeds for neighbors. In January, 1832 he agreed to draft an agreement between James Rutledge and David P. Nelson, which cleared up payment of an outstanding debt between them. The young man who drifted into to New Salem knowing no one was now an unofficial legal counsellor for many in the town.

Contrary to popular belief, it is clear that even at this early stage of life, Lincoln had ambition, talent, and the determination to make something of himself. He was no confused youth, struggling to find his way. He was actively pursuing an upward path.

He may have been striving to move upward, but the climb would not be without stumbles and falls. For months, Denton Offutt had been paying little attention to anything in New Salem but the barrels of Kentucky rye whiskey in his store. He was drinking heavily and ignoring his debts to suppliers and the unpaid bills accumulated by store patrons. Soon, with his reserves of cash nearly exhausted, he found it necessary to close up the store. Lincoln assumed responsibility for paying the debts owed to suppliers by Denton Offutt. He was not legally bound to do it, but he felt that it was the right thing to do.

Lincoln was once again out of steady work. Neighbors offered him odd jobs, and for a time he became regionally famous as the man who piloted a small steamboat, the Talisman, downriver to Beardstown. A group of businessmen had hired the boat to blaze a water trail from central Illinois to Cincinnati, on the Ohio River. From there goods would head east to Pittsburg, Pennsylvania. This would open up

eastern markets to the farmers of the West. **The Talisman** made it as far as Bogue's Mill, north of New Salem. It sat there for a week, halted by the low level of the Sangamon River. The investors decided to recall the ship, and hired Lincoln to guide her safely back downriver. Lincoln helped pilot the Talisman through narrow points in the river clogged with fallen logs and snags, and dangerously low water levels, to Beardstown, Illinois, where he disembarked, and walked back home. For his efforts he received $40 and much local acclaim as the resident expert on the navigability of the river so crucial to New Salem's future.

In March, 1832, only eight months after stepping ashore at New Salem, Lincoln announced that he was a candidate for the Illinois State Legislature from Sangamon County. In a speech he gave that was later printed as a handbill, he outlined his position on the issues of most concern to local citizens; the need for improvement of the Sangamon River to make it fully navigable for ships such as the Talisman; the need for building a system of canals and railroads to transport farmers goods to market; and laws to fix the limits of interest on loans (usury). He concluded his remarks on a personal note:

If the good people in their wisdom shall see fit to keep me in the background, I have been too familiar with disappointments to be very much chagrined.[4]

Before he could commence a proper campaign, war broke out on the Illinois frontier.

The Sauk and Fox Indians had lived in settlements along the Rock River in northern Illinois for hundreds of years, planting and harvesting their corn crops, hunting game, and fishing the many streams and rivers of the area. In 1804, after receiving promises that they could remain on their lands as long as that land remained property of the United States, the tribes ceded the land to the federal government. Almost immediately squatters began to move into the tribal lands, and arguments and hostilities broke out. In 1831 the Indians agreed to move west to Iowa, and not return without the permission of the Governor of Illinois or President of the United States.

Less than a year later **Black Hawk**, chief of the Sauk tribe, had changed his mind. He argued:

"My reason teaches me that land cannot be sold. The Great Spirit gave it to his children to live upon. So long as they occupy and cultivate it, they have a right to the soil. Nothing can be sold but such things as can be carried away.[5]

On April 5, 1832, Black Hawk returned to Illinois with 2,000 of his people, headed, for their old Rock River lands, to peacefully plant and harvest a corn crop, and then return to Iowa. 400 were mounted and well-armed, with the balance consisting of old men, women and young boys.[74] Word spread rapidly throughout Illinois. Governor Reynolds called for volunteers from the state militia to help drive Black Hawk and his people back across the Mississippi River to Iowa. At this time, all males age 18-45 were required to enroll in the militia, and failure to do so would lead to punishment as a deserter. Towns began calling up their local militiamen for thirty days service. Federal troops would eventually arrive to help quell the Indian uprising (as white men perceived it), but that would take some time. Meanwhile, local militia would defend the land.

New Salem's militia gathered on some flat ground near the center of town, and as their first order of business, elected officers. The Clary's Grove boys, who were numerous among the militiamen, helped elect Abraham Lincoln, who was not yet present, as Captain, with Jack Armstrong as his first sergeant. A soldier from a neighboring town, described Abraham Lincoln's mounted company of the 35th Regiment of Illinois Militia (about 40 men), as "the hardest set of men he ever saw." Even though they respected Lincoln, his company had little respect for military discipline. Upon issuing them his first order, he received the response of "Go to the devil."[6]

Black Hawk and his people proved to be an elusive prey. After a month of futile pursuit, Lincoln's company had still seen no Indians. His company passed its free time in camp with singing, foot races, and wrestling. Several companies put up their best men to grapple with Lincoln, and he beat them all until he finally was thrown by a soldier named Lorenzo Thompson at a camp in Beardstown, Illinois.

On May 14, 1832, near an area known as Old Man's Creek, a group of militia under the command of a Major Stillman, located Black Hawk's warriors. Under the orders from Governor Reynolds to drive the Indians off, they advanced against a band of 40 to 50 of Black Hawk's warriors, who were bearing a flag of truce. Black Hawk's warriors soundly defeated the soldiers, killing twelve men, and driving the rest from the field. The next day Lincoln and members of his company were ordered to the battle site to bury the bodies of the fallen soldiers. Lincoln came face to face with the reality of war when he and his detachment discovered twelve dead soldiers, scalped and mutilated, their swollen bodies swarming with flies, unrecognizable in the heat of the day.

Two weeks later, Lincoln's company was mustered out of service, its enlistment period ended. Lincoln immediately re-enlisted for twenty days with a company commanded by Captain Elijah Iles. The man who mustered him in, Second Lieutenant Robert Anderson, later became famous as the commander of Union forces at Fort Sumter, in the harbor of Charleston, South Carolina, where the first shots of the Civil War were fired.

Lincoln's new company marched northwest, toward Galena, Illinois, to scout for signs of Black Hawk's men, gathering intelligence along the way about their enemy's strength and intentions. Near Elizabethtown, Lincoln's enlistment again ran out, and once again he re-enlisted, this time with a spy company commanded by Captain Jacob Early. On June 25th they received a call for support from Major John Dement, at Kellogg's Grove. Dement's men had run into a large war party and been driven in disorder to an unoccupied cabin where they rallied and fought off repeated attacks, losing five men. Early's company found them there the next day, and learned that Black Hawk had left the area during the night.

After pursuing Black Hawk's warriors into what is now Wisconsin, (near present-day Fort Atkinson), Jacob Early's spy company, suffering from a lack of provisions, was disbanded, and Lincoln was honorably discharged from service. During the night, as he packed up in preparation to head home, Lincoln's horse and equipment were stolen.

The next morning Lincoln accepted an offer from George Harrison, a fellow Illinoisan, to ride with him on the man's horse for part of the 200 mile journey back to Peoria, Illinois. He and Harrison purchased a canoe there and made their way south, down the Illinois River. By July 17th Harrison and Lincoln arrived in Havana, Illinois, where they sold the canoe, and walked the rest of the way home.

Abraham Lincoln's time as a soldier was over. In two and a half months he had marched hundreds of miles all over northern Illinois, and experienced the trials and exhilaration of leading men for the first time. While he saw no combat and never fired a shot at the enemy, he did observe the chaos of war and the horror of its aftermath.

Years later, as a Congressman, Lincoln referred to his time in the Black Hawk War when the House of Representatives rang with laughter as he gave a speech ridiculing the greatly exaggerated war record of Democratic Senator Lewis Cass, then a Presidential candidate:

Mister Speaker, did you know I am a military hero? Yes sir; in the days of the Black Hawk War I fought, bled and came away. Speaking of General Cass's career reminds me of my own. I was not at Stillman's defeat, but I was about as near it as Cass was to Hull's surrender: and, like him, I saw the place very soon afterwards. It is quite certain I did not break my sword, for I had none to break, but I bent a musket pretty bad on one occasion. If Cass broke his sword, the idea is, he broke it in desperation. I broke my musket by accident. If General Cass went in advance of me in picking blueberries, I guess I surpassed him n charges upon the wild onions. If he saw any live, fighting Indian, it was more than I did, but I had a good many bloody struggles with the mosquitos, and, although I never fainted from loss of blood, I can truly say I was often hungry.[7]

***

By the time Abraham Lincoln returned to New Salem in late July, the campaign for the state legislature was in its final ten days. He began travelling all around his district, pigeon-holing voters wherever he could find them, trying to make up for lost time. At Pappsville, Illinois, before he could start speaking, a fight broke out. Lincoln stepped down from the platform, grabbed the instigator by the neck and seat of his trousers and flung the man several feet. That ended the fight, after which Lincoln commenced his talk.

I presume you all know who I am. I am humble Abraham Lincoln. I have been solicited by many friends to become a candidate for the Legislature. My politics are short and sweet, like the old woman's dance. I am in favor of a national bank. I am in favor of the internal improvement system and a high protective tariff. These are my sentiments and political principles. If elected I shall be thankful; if not, it will be all the same. [8]

A. Y. Ellis, a New Salem merchant, saw Lincoln during the campaign and described him:

I remember well how he was dressed. He wore flax and tow linen pantaloons – I thought about five inches too short in the legs – and frequently he had but one suspender, no vest or coat. He wore a calico shirt, such as he had in the Black Hawk War; coarse brogans, tan colored; blue yarn socks, and straw hat, old style, without a band.[9]

Thirteen candidates ran for four seats that would represent Lincoln's district in the state Legislature in 1832. He came in eighth, a respectable showing, considering that he was absent for most of the campaign. In his own precinct around New Salem he won 277 of the 300 votes cast, and this gave him hope for his future. It also caused the powers that be in the Whig party of the Illinois to take notice of this tall, rough- hewn young man, who only a year before had been a stranger to the area.

Lincoln, failing in his bid for a seat in the state legislature, found himself without a job. He considered becoming a blacksmith. He had the strength for it, but hesitated to be locked into a job that meant purely manual labor. He wanted to begin studying the law, but he feared that his lack of formal education would prove too great an obstacle to success in that field. Finally, an appealing alternative presented itself. There were three general stores in New Salem, one owned by John McNeill and Samuel Hill, another run by Rueben Radford, and a third run by William Berry and James Herndon. Berry had recently lost his partner, who had moved away. James Herndon had sold his part of the business to his brother Rowan. William Berry got Rowan to sell James' part of the business to Lincoln, who was, at that time, boarding with the Herndon's. Rowan told his cousin, Lincoln biographer William Herndon:

I believed he (Lincoln) was thoroughly honest, and that impression was so strong that I accepted his note in payment of the whole. He had no money, but

I would have advanced him still more had he asked for it.[10]

In January, 1833, Rueben Radford, store owner and competitor of William Berry, got into a disagreement with the Clary's Grove boys, who, as a result, broke the windows of his store and destroyed much of his stock. The discouraged Radford then sold his remaining stock, and the store itself, to Berry and Lincoln.

The partnership was doomed almost from the beginning. Berry, the son of a preacher, was a drunkard. Like Offutt before him, he did little more in their store than to consume its stock of whiskey. In March, 1833 Berry, probably without Lincoln's knowledge, obtained from the Sangamon County Commissioners Court, a license to sell spirits in quantities less than a quart. In those times most stores sold liquor in volumes no less than a quart, to be consumed off premises. A special license was required to sell smaller quantities that would be consumed on premises. These places were known as "groceries," and they were looked down upon by the upstanding members of most communities. The license that Berry obtained was signed with both his and Lincoln's name, but both were in Berry's handwriting.

Less than a month later, Lincoln sold Berry his part of the business, in return receiving a note of credit. Lincoln transferred the note of credit to those people he owed money to, to pay down part of his debts. Fortunately, Lincoln was still well liked and trusted in New Salem. He easily found work on neighboring farms, making a wage that would equal over $100 yearly, with free bed and meals. This was enough money to allow a man to purchase eighty acres of land if he chose to. Lincoln used his earnings to continue paying down the debts that he had taken on as a result of the failed Offutt-Lincoln store.

On January 10, 1835, **William Berry** died, probably from his excessive drinking. This meant that the notes he gave Lincoln for Lincoln's part of the store, and which Lincoln used to pay his own debts, were worthless. Lincoln would now have to make good on both his debt, and Berry's failed notes of credit. His "national debt," as he would later call it, would take him over a decade to pay off.

Pollard Simmons, a friend and neighbor of Lincoln, knew he was working hard to earn enough money to pay down his debts. Sometime in 1833 Pollard approached John Calhoun, who was the surveyor of Sangamon County, and asked him if he might consider appointing Abraham Lincoln as his deputy. Though he was a Democrat, and Lincoln a Whig, Calhoun agreed. When Pollard told Lincoln of the appointment, Lincoln hesitated, asking Pollard, "Do I have to give up any of my principles for this job? If I have to surrender any thought or principle to get it I wouldn't touch it with a ten foot pole."[81] Pollard assured him that the job was strictly a surveying job, and politics would not be involved.

Lincoln's surveying work was not bringing in much money, and, added to the money he earned working odd jobs on local farms, he was not making enough to provide himself with a living wage. In May of 1833, the women of New Salem, upset with their treatment by the post-master of the town, Samuel Hill, petitioned to have Hill removed from office. It seems that when they would come to his store to pick up their mail, Hill would ignore them, while selling liquor to his male patrons. Hill was removed, and on May 7, 1833, after lobbying from his friends in town, Lincoln was appointed postmaster. The position, once again, was awarded to him by Democrats. When asked how he, a loyal Whig, could get such a patronage appointment from the opposing party, Lincoln explained that the position of postmaster of New Salem was "too insignificant to make his politics an objection."[11]

So we find Abraham Lincoln, at age 24; well liked in his community, having clerked at a store that went bankrupt, having owned a store that failed because of the constant inebriation of his partner, having lost a campaign for the state legislature, having run up a large (almost $1,000 in 1833) debt, and living off jobs gotten for him by those who, despite his setbacks, believed him capable, trustworthy, and deserving of better things.

Despite his rough handling by life up to this point, his neighbors recalled him as being a young man of wit, with winning ways, but bad luck. Mrs. Elizabeth Abell, in whose home Lincoln sometimes stayed, said of him during these days:

I never considered him so (a sad man). He was always social and lively and had great aspirations for his friends, always decided and good natured.[12]

Darkness seems not to have overtaken him yet.

***

1834 was a pivotal and very busy year in the life of Abraham Lincoln. He was serving as postmaster of New Salem, and doing work as deputy surveyor for the northern part of Sangamon County. On April

4, 1834, his name appeared in the "Sangamo Journal" newspaper as a candidate for the state legislature. He campaigned hard this time, giving numerous speeches all over his central Illinois district. His service in the Black Hawk War, and the many citizens he met while performing his surveying and postmaster duties, gave him high name recognition. On August 4, 1834, he was elected, running second out of twelve candidates (the top four vote getters received legislative seats).

He missed first place by fourteen votes.

In December, 1834, the man whose earlier dreams were of a life working on the Ohio River took his seat in the Illinois legislature, located in the **state capitol, Vandalia, Illinois**. He spent the next several months learning the intricacies of legislative work, and meeting some of the leading statesmen of Illinois; Benjamin Bond, brother of the state's first governor, Thomas Owen, one of the first trustees of Chicago, John Vance, a wealthy salt manufacturer, and Stephen A. Douglas. Douglas was an ambitious young Democrat, who mesmerized crowds with his powerful baritone voice, combative debate style and sharp logic. He had a barrel chest and huge head that seemed out of place set atop a pair of very short legs. After his first meeting with Douglas, who would play a key role during the rest of his days in Illinois, Lincoln called him "the least man" he had ever seen.

John T. Stuart, a fellow member of the legislature and leading attorney in Springfield, Illinois, urged Lincoln to begin studying the law. Lincoln's earlier misgivings about his deficient schooling being an impediment to success at the bar seemed to have disappeared. Lincoln borrowed several volumes of law texts from Stuart and began to pour over them like a man possessed, or perhaps, a man in love who had finally caught sight of his future.

William Kolasinski

Chapter Six

ANN RUTLEDGE
Romance or Rumor?

One villager that Lincoln looked forward to seeing when she came in to pick up her family's mail at the post office located in Samuel Hill's store was Ann Rutledge. Ann was living with her father at his inn and tavern, helping with cooking and cleaning and waiting on lodgers and store patrons. Lincoln had been lodging there for some time after coming to New Salem, and had ample opportunity to make her acquaintance.

There are several descriptions of Ann given by those who knew her. James Short, who lived near the Rutledge's, said of her:

Miss Rutledge was a good-looking, smart, lively girl, a good housekeeper, with a moderate education, and without any of the so-called accomplishments.[1]

Her fiancée, John McNeill (his real name was later discovered to be McNamar) said:

Miss Ann was a gentle, amiable maiden, without any of the airs of your city belles, but winsome and comely withal; a blonde in complexion, with golden hair, cherry-red lips, and a bonny blue eye.[2]

Mrs. Hardin Bale, a close friend of Ann's, said that

She had auburn hair, blue eyes, fair complexion; was a slim, pretty, kind, tender, good-hearted woman; in height about five feet three inches, and weighed about one hundred and twenty pounds. She was beloved by all who knew her.[3]

Parthena Nance Hill, who married Samuel Hill after Ann rejected his proposal of marriage, saw Ann in the less flattering light of a competitor for the attentions of the eligible bachelors of New Salem. When asked by William Herndon for a description of her, Mrs. Hill said:

Ann Rutledge had brown hair, and was heavy set.[4]

Ann had been courted by two of the leading citizens of the community, Samuel Hill and John McNeill. This must have made for some rough times for them both, as they were partners in the biggest store in New Salem. Hill proposed to Ann first, and was rejected. McNeill pressed his suit and Ann accepted his proposal. Hill, angered by McNeill's success in love where he had failed, grew combative and abusive in his relations with his partner, and eventually McNeill agreed to sell his share in the store to Hill. McNeill then told Ann why he came to New Salem. He explained to her that his real name was McNamar, and that he left his home state of New York and travelled west to New Salem to escape his family's relatives, who were poor and constantly hounding him and his parents for financial help. He intended to make a fortune in New Salem, so that he could provide for his mother and father. He told her that he had to leave New Salem and return to New York to set his parents up to live comfortably. Then he would return to New Salem and marry Ann. She was shocked at first, but respected his commitment to his parents.

McNeill used some of the proceeds from the sale of his share of the Hill-McNeill store to purchase a forty acre farm in nearby Sandridge, Illinois, and told Ann that she and her family could live there until he returned. He then bid her a sad farewell, promising again that he would be back in three months, and they would then be wed.

Lincoln knew that Ann was engaged, and he liked McNeill, so he kept his relationship with Ann friendly and platonic. Months past, and Ann began receiving letters from McNeill less frequently. For a long period, they stopped completely. Ann did not know what to think. Lincoln watched as Ann came to his post office daily, sometimes twice daily, to see if there were any letters for her from McNeill. **He was drawn to Ann,** but, out of friendship for McNeill, he remained no more than a good friend who commiserated with her sad situation.

Neighbors began to gossip that McNeill had played her falsely, and she began to think so as well. Ann had recently moved away from New Salem to the farm that John McNeill had purchased for them before he left for New York. Lincoln now began to court Ann, but this was not evident to the citizens of the area, as the Rutledge farm was far out of town, on the prairie. So far as the citizens of New Salem were concerned, Lincoln was only her friend, and she was still engaged to John McNeill. **Ann** confided to her brother David that she planned to confront McNeill upon his return to New Salem, and ask to be released from the engagement. She had grown close to Abraham Lincoln during McNeill's absence, and they had made plans for a life together. She would attend Jacksonville Female Academy, and Lincoln would complete his studies and set up in business practicing law. Upon her graduation from the Academy they would marry. David urged her to write McNeill immediately, informing him that she no longer loved him and considered the engagement ended. Ann refused, insisting that the proper thing to do was to give him the news in person.[5]

Months of work in the legislature kept Lincoln away from home and Ann Rutledge. She passed the time doing farm chores with her mother, quilting (at which she was reputed to be very skillful), and preparing to attend school. The legislature adjourned on February 13, 1835, and Lincoln returned home to New Salem. Over the next several months, according to James (Uncle Jimmy) Short, who lived very close to the Rutledge's Sandridge farm, Lincoln visited the Rutledge's several times a week. Lincoln and Ann probably spent their time together discussing her upcoming enrollment at Jacksonville Academy, and his experiences in Vandalia.[6] Ann was determined to receive an education befitting the wife of a prominent and rising politician.

Ann never learned what had kept John McNeil (McNamar) from returning to Illinois. He had returned to New York after a journey that was longer and more difficult than he had expected. He had lost some time when he was forced to remain in bed at a wayside inn along the route east, battling a high fever. When he finally resumed his journey and reached his parent's home, he discovered that his father was dying, sick and broken from financial difficulties. Other members of his family also fell ill during the days he was in New York, further delaying his departure back to Illinois. He did write to Ann about some of these difficulties, but his letters were more infrequent than she hoped, and their tone grew less and less intimate.

In mid-July, Ann fell ill. William Herndon described her condition:

Late in the summer she took to her bed. A fever was burning in her head, Day by day she sank, until all hope was banished. During the latter days of her sickness, her physician had forbidden visitors to enter her room, prescribing absolute quiet. But her brother relates that she kept inquiring for

Lincoln so continuously, at times demanding to see him, that the family at last sent for him. On his arrival at her bedside the door was closed and he was left alone with her. What was said, what vows and revelations were made during this sad interview, were known only to him and the dying girl. A few days afterward she became unconscious and remained so until her death.[7]

During the days of Ann's illness, Lincoln was staying at the home of Dr. Bennett Abell and his wife Elizabeth. They had a comfortable cabin set atop a small hill just south of the town of Petersburg, a few miles from the Rutledge farm. Mrs. Abell commented on Lincoln's behavior following the death of Ann:

...it was a great shock to him, and I never seen a man mourn for a companion more than he did for her. He made a remark one day when it was raining that he could not bear the idea of its raining on her grave. That was the time when the community said he was crazy. He was not crazy, but he was very disponding a long time.[8]

Grave of Ann Rutledge, Concord Cemetery.

In the days following Ann's burial, Lincoln made regular pilgrimages to her gravesite in the old **Concord Cemetery**, a lonely piece of ground, far enough away from any civilization to be completely silent, but for the winds rustling through the trees shading her resting place. Here he would lay down, his arm resting on the mound of earth that covered her, weeping and speaking words only he could hear.

***

There is an ongoing debate among historians about the real nature of the relationship between Ann Rutledge and Abraham Lincoln. Following the President's assassination in 1865, William Herndon began conducting interviews with those people who knew Lincoln, in preparation for writing a biography of his law partner's life. Lincoln's New Salem friends and neighbors each related bits and pieces of their recollection of his time spent in their village, and it became apparent that they believed that Lincoln loved Ann Rutledge. Herndon, in 1866, gave a lecture on the subject, which shocked and enraged Mary Todd Lincoln and her family. She insisted that she was the President's true and only love, and that the Rutledge name had never once been mentioned by him during their courtship and marriage. The public, however, embraced the romantic idea of the simple prairie boy falling in love and suffering a tragic loss. For many years it was repeated by biographers as a crucial part of the Lincoln story.

In the 1960's, the great Lincoln biographer J. G. Randall, in an appendix to his four volume work, attacked the story, refuting it in scholarly detail. The crux of his argument was that Herndon interviewed people 30 years after the affair, and used leading questions to solicit the story he wanted. Randall pointed out that Herndon's informants were old and their memories were unreliable, their recollections unsupported by provable fact. Randall was a man greatly admired by Lincoln scholars for his meticulous research, and as a result of his work, the Rutledge-Lincoln story soon became no more than a pleasant fiction to many who went on to write new biographies of Lincoln.

In the 1990's, fresh research began to shed new light on the Rutledge-Lincoln relationship. John E. Walsh's book, "The Shadows Rise, Abraham Lincoln and the Ann Rutledge Legend" and Douglas

Wilson's book, "Lincoln Before Washington", both utilized the actual written notes Herndon took when questioning Lincoln's friends and neighbors (something Randall never did, as they were not yet available to the public then). Those notes indicate that Herndon did not lead his witness's testimony. They provided their information about Lincoln and Ann Rutledge to Herndon without prompting by him. And Herndon attempted to verify their comments by comparing them and questioning each person as to why their recollection might not agree exactly with another person. He was clearly surprised by what he was hearing, and was digging to get at the common threads of truth that ran through the many stories he was hearing.

The version I have told is consistent with the finding of Walsh and Wilson. Ann Rutledge and Abraham Lincoln did have a strong relationship, and probably were, unknown to the general public, secretly engaged.

To balance things, let me first quote from a statement that Isaac Cogdal gave William Herndon during an interview after Lincoln's death, in which he related a meeting he had with Lincoln in Springfield after Lincoln had been elected President, and before he left for his inauguration. He and Lincoln had been friends in New Salem, and Lincoln in the late 1850's had encouraged Cogdal to study law. He said that Lincoln had invited him to stop by his offices after sundown, when all other visitors would be gone. When Cogdal arrived, Lincoln started the conversation:

I want to enquire about old times and old acquaintances. When we lived in Salem there were the Greenes, the Potters, Armstrongs, and Rutledges. These folks have got scattered all over the world – some are dead.[9]

Cogdal and Lincoln discussed their mutual friends, where they were living currently and how they were doing. When he felt that Lincoln was warming to the subject of their old days together, he decided to carefully ask a very personal question. He asked if Lincoln would respond to such a question, and Lincoln replied that if it was fair, he would "with all his heart," do his best to respond.

This is the exchange that followed.

Cogdale: Abe, is it true that you fell in love with and courted Ann Rutledge?

Lincoln: It is true indeed. I have loved the name of Rutledge to this day. I have kept my mind on their movements ever since and love them dearly.

Cogdale: Abe, is it true that you ran a little wild about the matter?

Lincoln: I did really – I run off the track; it was my first. I loved the woman dearly and sacredly: she was a handsome girl – would have made a good loving wife – was natural and quite intellectual, though not highly educated – I did honestly and truly love the girl and think often – often of her now.

Cogdal was close to Lincoln and had no score to settle or axe to grind. He did not attempt to widely publicize this exchange. He only revealed it upon being questioned by William Herndon.

The last word goes to Mary Todd Lincoln. Surely Lincoln's wife, if anyone, would know if his heart had been given to someone before her. After William Herndon gave a lecture in 1866, revealing for the first time his "evidence" of Lincoln's love for Ann Rutledge, Mary Lincoln was quick to respond to him:

He is a dirty dog. For I have friends, if his low soul thought that my great affliction left me without them.[10]

She insisted that Lincoln had many times assured her that she was the only woman he had ever cared for, and that she had never, in their entire life together, ever heard the name Ann Rutledge mentioned. She concluded:

Nor did his life or joyous laugh lead one to suppose his heart was in any unfortunate woman's grave, but in the proper place with his loved wife and children.[11]

***

The story of Abraham Lincoln's love for Ann Rutledge is crucial in attempting to understand how he became the man we know. Before Ann's death he was a man on the rise, a man known for his easy humor and hearty, whole body laugh. People sought to be in his company. Following Ann's untimely death, he was a different man, brooding, close mouthed, unwilling to open up his thoughts to even his closest friends. A shadow had begun to fall over him, one that caused him to begin to speak frequently of death, even suicide.

William Kolasinski

Chapter Seven

LOSS, LOVE, THE LEGISLATURE AND LAW

Following Ann Rutledge's death, many of Lincoln's friends feared what his deep grief might drive him to do. He was given lodging at the home of Judge Bowling Green and his wife Nancy, who lived in a spacious cabin located just below the bluff that was crowned by the town of New Salem. Lincoln loved the old couple. New Salem neighbors like Abner Ellis considered Judge Green to be like Lincoln's second father. For weeks Lincoln remained despondent, barely talking to the Greens or any friends or neighbors who stopped by to try to lift him from his despair. The Greens watched over him, carefully removing any sharp objects lying about from his sight. One evening, while staring out the window into the darkness of a night misted with cold rain, Mrs. Green heard him say to himself, "I can't bear to think of her out there alone," and then, moments later, with clenched fists, "The rain and storm shan't beat on her grave."[1]

***

Lincoln slowly regained his emotional balance, and returned to work. On September 24, 1835, barely a month after Ann's death, he was out of the Green's cabin conducting a survey near New Salem.[2] On December 7, 1835 he was back in the state capital, Vandalia, for a brief, special session of the legislature. He then returned to New Salem and spent two months surveying the plat for the new town of Petersburg, just seven miles to the north.

His term of office was coming to an end, so in early March, 1836, he announced his candidacy for re-election. He found escape from recent grieving by campaigning extensively throughout his district. His hard work was rewarded when, in August, 1836, a year after Ann's death, he came in first out of 17 candidates for the four seats available to his district in the legislature.

***

The personal trauma he had suffered caused him to think more about his religious beliefs. He had begun as a Baptist, adopting his parents' beliefs. By his 27th year, that had changed. While living in New Salem he had become a member of the debating society, where he met many well-read people who held very liberal views on religion. They read and discussed the poetry of Robert Burns, Edward Gibbon's Rise and Fall of The Roman Empire, and the political sentiments of Thomas Paine. In Scottish poet Robert Burns Lincoln probably recognized a man like himself, who began life as a poor farm boy, moody, tending to depression, who enjoyed a bawdy joke or rhyme. Burns was alienated from organized religion. Reading Gibbon's history of Rome, he learned of the author's conviction that Christianity caused the mighty city's downfall. When he read Thomas Paine's Age of Reason, he may have found sympathy with the author's proclaimed new creed:

I believe in one God, and no more; and I hope for happiness beyond this life. I believe in the equality of man; and I believe that religious duties consist in doing justice, loving mercy, and endeavoring to make our fellow creatures happy.[2]

Whether he read these authors' works because they supported what he already thought, or whether reading them influenced him to accept their philosophies is not clear, but whatever the case, he became known around New Salem and among his wide circle of friends as "an infidel."

William Herndon, in notes he recorded from an 1866 interview with James Matheny (best man at Lincoln's wedding), quoted him speaking about Lincoln in the late 1830's:

...when all were idle and nothing to do, would talk about religion – pick up the Bible – read a passage – and then comment on it – show its falsity – and its follies on the grounds of reason – would then show its own self-made and self-uttered contradictions and would in the end – finally ridicule it and as it were scoff at it.[3]

Lincoln was not alone in holding such beliefs, but for a public man, a man who had to stand for office asking for the votes of thousands of believers, it was a dangerous set of beliefs if made public.

Sometime in 1835 or 1836, Lincoln sought to do just that. He wrote a pamphlet spelling out his religious beliefs. When his friends heard of his intentions to publish the pamphlet, they urged him not to, assuring him that it would mean the end of his career in politics. Lincoln remained adamant, and as he read his writings to Samuel Hill, the New Salem storekeeper, Hill snatched it from his hands and threw it into the stove, whose flames consumed it immediately. Lincoln could have rewritten it, but he did not. He was angry, but must have come to realize the wisdom of what his friend Hill had done. He did not change his beliefs; he simply chose not to make them public in the future.

The difficulty of his childhood, his strained relationship with his father, and the death of so many he had loved, all had led him far away from his parents' acceptance of organized religion and Jesus Christ as the Son of God.

***

Robert Wilson, a fellow member of the legislature representing the Sangamon District, lived in Athens, Illinois, near New Salem. Lincoln visited him there frequently, usually staying for a day or two.

They would visit the local stores and meet with their constituents, gauging public sentiment on issues before the legislature. Townsfolk always gathered quickly wherever Lincoln and Wilson stopped. Lincoln would lean against a wall, plop his huge booted foot (size thirteen) onto a box to steady himself, and then regale them with story after story, laughing at the punchlines as hard as anyone in the crowd did. In a lengthy letter to William Herndon in 1866, Wilson spoke of a conversation he had with Lincoln when he was in Athens in 1836:

He told me that although he appeared to enjoy life rapturously, still he was the victim of terrible melancholy. He sought company, and indulged in fun and hilarity without restraint, or stint as to time. Still, when by himself, he told me that he was so overcome with mental depression that he never dared carry a knife in his pocket. And as long as I was intimately acquainted with him, previous to his commencement of the practice of law, he never carried a pocket knife.[4]

Some of the people Herndon interviewed following Lincoln's death attributed this prolonged depression to mental exhaustion brought on by him overworking himself; trying to conduct surveys, do his job as a legislator, and spend hours studying law books. I believe those contributed to his mental state, in addition to his grief over the loss of Ann Rutledge. The shadow that darkened Lincoln's psyche had descended, and would never fully leave him.

***

The New Salem post office closed in May, 1836. It had never done much business, but Lincoln did receive a $75 lump sum payment in wages from the government based on the amount of mail he had handled as postmaster.

He began to work on a scheme to promote a navigable canal along the Sangamon River that would connect the New Salem area with Beardstown Illinois, on the Illinois River. This canal, he argued, would allow area farmers to transport their goods from central Illinois to Beardstown, then down the Illinois River to the Mississippi River and all the way to New Orleans, quicker and cheaper than by any then- current routes. He joined with a Beardstown businessman named Francis Arenz and several residents of New Salem and Petersburg, creating and buying shares in the canal company.

I mention this episode because it reinforces the possibility that Lincoln may have consorted with a prostitute while staying in Beardstown, Illinois on business. William Herndon recorded notes of a conversation he had with Lincoln in the 1850's, during which Lincoln admitted to the liaison. Herndon later claimed that he never meant for the notes to be made public. In the late 1860's, he had loaned a small notebook to Ward Hill Lamon that contained pages of interviews and recollections, as part of a larger group of materials intended to help Lamon write a biography of Lincoln. Herndon did not realize the notebook contained that sensitive information until Lamon published it in his biography of Lincoln in 1872

There is evidence to speculate that Lincoln may have been afraid that he contracted syphilis during this encounter with a prostitute. Half the men of Lincoln's day had some form of sexually transmitted disease. Fear of sexual disease was a typical feature of what physicians of that day called hypochondriasis. That worry would have added to his already gloomy disposition, and might explain his irrational behavior in the next romantic attachment he formed.

***

In November of 1836, the sister of Lincoln's good friend, Mrs. Elizabeth Abell, travelled to New Salem for a visit. She had been there in 1833, when she and Lincoln first met. Lincoln found her then to be an intelligent and "handsome woman." Following Ann Rutledge's death, Mrs. Abell thought it would be beneficial for Lincoln to consider courting again, and suggested that her sister, Mary Owens, would be a suitable match. Mrs. Abell would contact her sister, telling her of Lincoln's interest in marriage, and if upon meeting and getting to know each they found themselves agreeable, a

marriage would take place. It was not unusual at the time for a marriage to be arranged in this way. Lincoln gave her his permission to have **Mary Owens** come to town.

More than a year had passed since Ann Rutledge's death, and Lincoln, at age 27, had desires as any man of that age would. The Beardstown affair, occurring around this time, showed that he had the passions any man might have. Lincoln's neighbor James Short told William Herndon this story, which he said Lincoln himself told many times.

Once, when Mr. Lincoln was surveying, he was put to bed in the same room with two girls, the head of his bed being next to the foot of the girls' bed. In the night he commenced to tickling the feet of one of the girls with his fingers. As she seemed to enjoy it as much as he did he then tickled a little higher up; and as he would tickle higher the girl would shove down lower and the higher he tickled the lower she moved. Mr. L would tell the story with evident enjoyment. He never told how that thing ended.[5]

The prospect that an intelligent and handsome, if not attractive, woman might consider marrying him seems to have appealed to him.

Mary Owens and Lincoln courted for over a year. He visited her at her sister's house, and attended several parties and gatherings with her. Finally, in 1838, he proposed, and to his shock, she said no. Mary Owens told her sister that Lincoln was, *"deficient in those little links which make up the great chain of a woman's happiness."* [6]

She gave William Herndon an example of Lincoln's deficient attentions to her.

There was a company of us going up to Uncle Billy Green's. Mr. L. was riding with me, and we had a very bad branch to cross. The other gentlemen

96

were very officious in seeing that their partners got over safely; we were behind, he riding and never looking back to see how I got along; when I rode back up to him, I remarked, you are a nice fellow, I suppose you did not care whether my neck was broken or not. He laughingly replied (I suppose by way of compliment), that he knew I was plenty smart enough to take care of myself.[7]

On April 1, 1838, Lincoln explained his side if the story. It was April fool's Day, and his biting comments might be partially attributed to his attempt at sarcastic humor, but his hurt and confusion are clear in the letter that he wrote that day to Mrs. Eliza Browning, a confidante, and the wife of his good friend, Orville Browning, telling of his courtship of Mary Owens.

I had seen said sister (Mary Owens was the sister of Elizabeth Abell) some three years before, thought her intelligent and agreeable, and saw no good objection to plodding through life with her.[8]

He then told of meeting her again, in 1836,

I knew she was over-size, but she now appeared a fair match for Falstaff.[9]

He said that she reminded him of his mother.

From her want of teeth, weather-beaten appearance in general, and from a kind of notion that ran in my head, that nothing could have commenced at the size of infancy, and reached her present bulk in less than thirty-five or forty years (Mary was then twenty-eight years old). But what could I do? I had told her sister that I would take her for better or worse; and I made a point of honor and conscience in all things, to stick to my word, especially if others had been induced to act on it, which, in this case, I doubted not they had, for I was now fairly convinced that no other man on earth would have her, and hence the conclusion that they were bent on holding me to my bargain.[10]

He concluded the letter explaining his disappointment and confusion over the whole affair.

My vanity was deeply wounded by the reflection, that I had so long been too stupid to discover her intentions, and at the same time never doubting that I understood them perfectly; and also that she whom I had taught myself to believe nobody else would ever have, had actually rejected me with all my fancied greatness, and to cap the whole, I then, for the first time, began to suspect that I was really a little in love with her.[11]

It is clear that Lincoln did not want to go through life alone, and that he was willing to accept Mary Owens, bad bargain though she might be, if for no other reason than his honor. Yet in the courtship he did everything he could to drive her away. Was he, in the end, fearful of what intimacy with a woman might reveal? Could a fear of recurring syphilitic symptoms have caused him to unconsciously sabotage the romance?

***

Lincoln was hard at work in the Illinois legislature during the 1836-1837 sessions, trying to create an Internal Improvement System for the state and arguing for movement of the capitol from Vincennes, in southern Illinois, to a more central location in the growing town of Springfield. His attempt to improve the infrastructure of Illinois mirrored the politics of his political idol, Henry Clay, who championed just such a system for the United States as a whole. Lincoln, like Clay, believed that if waterways were improved and railroads were expanded, then farmers would see the cost of shipping their goods to market decrease, thereby increasing their profits. In January of 1837 the legislature passed a series of bills authorizing the start of these improvements in the state. Debate continued on how to fund the enterprise. In February of 1837, the legislature approved relocating the capitol to Springfield. One of these bills would bring Lincoln honors and accolades from his constituents, the other would come back to haunt Lincoln and his Whig Party.

While he was still in the midst of his courtship of Mary Owens, Abraham Lincoln left the little town on the bluff of the Sangamon River and moved to Springfield, Illinois. His desire for personal growth could no longer be satisfied in little New Salem. He accepted an offer to be the junior partner of John T. Stuart, a leading attorney in the growing town of Springfield, and moved there on April 15, 1837.

The day he arrived in Springfield, Lincoln stopped at a grocery and inquired of the clerk, **Joshua Speed**, where he might find a place to board. Speed told him of several establishments that could provide him shelter, but when Lincoln heard what that would cost, he was shocked. As always, he was nearly broke. Speed felt sorry for him and offered to let Lincoln sleep in his room upstairs above the store, until he could gather enough money to find better lodgings. They would have to share the same bed, which was not at all unusual in the 19th century. Lincoln walked outside to his horse, removed a saddlebag, carried it up into the attic space above the store, dropped the bag there, returned to the main floor, and smiled broadly at the clerk as he announced, "Well, Speed, I am moved."

***

John Todd Stuart and Abraham Lincoln worked many cases together in the coming months, with an increasing load falling on the shoulders of Lincoln, the firm's junior partner. Stuart was busy campaigning against Stephen A. Douglas for a seat in Congress.

With his notoriety as one of the men responsible for getting Springfield declared the new state capitol, Lincoln was much in demand as a speaker. In

January of 1838, he spoke before the Springfield Young Men's Lyceum. Months earlier, an anti-abolition mob had murdered an anti-slavery newspaper editor, Elijah Lovejoy, in Alton, Illinois. The violence had shocked the people of the state. Lincoln chose as the subject of his address the need for reason, not passion, in political and public discourse. His speech that day shows that his style had not yet evolved into the lean, lyrical style it would later be.

Lincoln spoke of his generation's duty to perpetuate those political institutions that our founding fathers had toiled to shape and fought to maintain. He asked the audience how they were going to do it.

How then, shall we perform it? At what point shall we expect the approach of danger? By what means shall we fortify against it? Shall we expect some transatlantic military giant to step the oceans, and crush us at a blow? Never! All the armies of Europe, Asia and Africa combined, with all the treasure of the earth in their military chest; with a Bonaparte for a commander, could not by force take a drink from the Ohio, or make a track on the Blue Ridge, in a trial of a thousand years.

I answer, if it ever reaches us it must spring up from amongst us. It cannot come from abroad. If destruction be our lot, we must ourselves be its author and finisher. As a nation of free men, we must live through all time or die by suicide.

I hope I am over-wary; but if I am not, there is, even now, something of an ill-omen amongst us. I mean the increasing disregard for law which pervades the country; the growing disposition to substitute the wild and furious passions, in lieu of the sober judgements of the courts; and the worse than savage mobs, for the executive ministers of justice.

Passion has helped us; but can do so no more...Reason, cold, calculating, unimpassioned reason, must furnish all the materials for our future support and defense. [13]

We can read in these lines the development of his power of reason and rhetoric, and also glimpse the horrors the nation would face in his lifetime. In our own times, with the ugly political discourse we hear daily over the radio and television, his thoughts are still relevant.

In the late spring, Lincoln's law partner and candidate for Congress, John Stuart, fell ill. It was nothing serious, but it prevented him from attending scheduled speaking engagements. Despite an already heavy workload of law cases and running himself for re-election to the Illinois legislature, Lincoln left Springfield and hit the campaign trail, speaking on behalf of Stuart and against Stuart's opponent, Stephen A. Douglas, who was becoming known as "The Little Giant."

Stuart recovered quickly, and continued the heated contest with Douglas for a seat in the U.S. House of Representatives. On August 6, 1838, both Lincoln and Stuart were rewarded by the voters for their efforts with victories, though not by impressive margins. Stuart won by only 36 votes out of over 36,000 cast. Lincoln amassed the lowest vote total of the four candidates who won seats in the legislature from the Sangamon district, his worst showing since his first attempt at the office. He was hurt by the effects of a national recession that had begun in 1837, which forced banks all around the country to close and spurred surging unemployment and food riots. The Internal Improvement System that Lincoln had fought for in the legislature had caused the state to run up a debt of $6.5 million dollars, at a time when state revenues only equaled $150,000 annually[14]. Lincoln had argued that though a debt would be incurred, the state could pay it down with the increases in revenue it would realize due to increased trade. The recession thwarted that trade growth, greatly expanded the state debt, and left Lincoln and the state Whig Party open to ridicule and calls for an investigation from opposing Democrats, who labelled them as financially irresponsible.

Overworked by shouldering all of the law firm's workload while travelling all over central Illinois campaigning, and embarrassed by the failure of his grand plan for state improvement, Lincoln began to fall into depression.

Two weeks later, an unsigned poem appeared in pages of the "Sangamo Journal" titled Suicide's Soliloquy. A note preceded the verse, explaining that the poem was found "near the bones" of an apparent suicide near the banks of the Sangamon River. There is no definitive proof that Lincoln wrote the poem, but scholars agree that its style is remarkably similar to other verses authored by Lincoln. Also, Joshua Speed, in interviews with William Herndon in the 1860's, insisted that Lincoln had told him of a poem about suicide that he wrote and submitted to the "Sangamo Journal" around this time.

The verses describe a person racked with thoughts self-destruction.

To ease me of this power to think,

That through my bosom raves,

I'll headlong leap from hell's high brink

And wallow in its waves.

It also strangely mirrors a letter Lincoln sent in 1842, to comfort a friend in the midst of a severe depression. In that letter Lincoln wrote about

That intensity of thought, which will sometimes wear the sweetest idea threadbare and turn it into the bitterness of death.[15]

The poem concludes:

Sweet steel! Come forth from out your sheath,

And glist'ning, speak your powers;

Rip up the organs of my breath,

And draw my blood in showers!

I strike! It quivers in that heart

Which draws me to this end;

I draw and kiss the bloody dart,

My last – my only friend.[16]

The poem was submitted anonymously to the "Sangamo Journal" for publication of August 25, 1838, the third anniversary of Ann Rutledge's death.

***

State and national politics dominated Lincoln's life during the early months of 1839, along with many cases that Stuart and Lincoln were arguing for their clients in court houses scattered across central Illinois' Eighth Judicial Circuit. "Riding the circuit" was an exhausting business. Lodgings were crowded and dirty, with three lawyers sometimes having to share one bed. Food was plain at best, and often barely edible. But the camaraderie the itinerant lawyers shared on these evenings spent around the fireplace was something that appealed to Lincoln. He was a favorite of all the lawyers and judges he met along the circuit, and they carried the stories and jokes he told back to their own home towns, where they circulated for years.

In the state legislature, Lincoln was trying to make the best of an awful situation, continuing to argue that the Internal Improvement System the Whigs had championed would, in the end, be a benefit to Illinois. If you make a bad bargain, he would often say, then hug it all the harder.

In February, 1839, the Whig Party of Illinois held a meeting to begin planning the campaign they would wage across the state in coming months for the election of William Henry Harrison to the Presidency. Lincoln was chosen as an elector (to cast his vote in the Electoral College if the Whigs won the state) for Harrison, and as one of several key spokesmen to carry Harrison's message to the people of Illinois. He was now recognized as a major player in state Whig politics, and as a very effective stump speaker. He worked very hard in coming months, speaking all over the state to assure a Harrison victory in Illinois.

Once Springfield became the state's capitol, the city had begun to grow, and attract young ladies in search of marriageable men. Ninian Edwards, son of a former Governor of the state, lived with his wife, Elizabeth Todd Edwards, in a mansion on Aristocrat's Hill, where the current capitol building now stands. Mrs. Edwards had several younger sisters living in her hometown of Lexington, Kentucky, and she invited them, one at a time, to come and visit her in Springfield, where they might find a proper mate to marry. Mrs. Edwards plotting to marry off her sisters bore fruit in May of 1839, when her sister Frances married Dr. William Wallace. When Frances moved out of the mansion, Mrs. Edwards sent a letter to her sister Mary, asking her to come and stay with her in Springfield. Mary Todd came to Springfield late in 1839. As a young girl Mary had announced that the man she married would someday be President of the United States. She was certain that she could find just such a man amongst the bachelors who populated her sister's soirees.

Chapter Eight
FINDING HIS PATH

After years of trying one path, then another, to earn a living for himself and to gain the esteem of his peers, Abraham Lincoln must have felt in 1839 that he had finally found the right path forward in life. He was a lawyer, a three term state legislator, a leader of his state's Whig Party, and a man well known and respected in his new home town of Springfield. He enjoyed the company of his good friend Joshua Speed, and the guidance of his senior law partner, Congressman John T. Stuart. His future, once clouded and uncertain, now seemed to be coming into focus. He was moving in the right direction, except in love.

The pain of Ann Rutledge's death was duller now, and the embarrassment he had felt over how he acted in the Mary Owens affair had faded. He knew that a man of thirty-two years, with his ambitions, needed to marry and start a family if he was to maintain the respect and trust of his fellow townsmen.

There was a group of bachelors in Springfield, known as "the Coterie," who regularly attended all the major social events in town where they might find a pretty girl willing to dance with them, flirt, with them, even marry them if the attraction was mutual. Lincoln was a member of that group. His friend Joshua Speed was another, who most of the ladies considered to be a real player with hearts. E.B. Webb was an older widower with two children, looking for a new mate. The group also included several Whig politicians: John J. Hardin, a handsome lawyer and native Kentuckian; Edward Baker, a friend and party rival of Lincoln's; James Matheny, son of the powerful Clerk of Sangamon County; and James C. Conkling. Two prominent Democrats rounded out the group: Stephen A. Douglas, recent loser to John T. Stuart in a race for Congress and currently Registrar of the Land Office but aiming for greater heights; and James Shields, a short, brash, thin skinned Irishman, currently in the state legislature with Lincoln. The Coterie regularly attended balls, cotillions, picnics and an occasional train excursion to parties in nearby Jacksonville, Illinois, to court the single ladies of central Illinois. In December, 1840, Lincoln, sent a jocular "petition" to the wife of his good friend, Orville H. Browning, requesting her to "repair forthwith to the Seat of Government, bringing in your train all ladies in general, who may be at your command." The petition was endorsed by several other members of the Coterie.

***

Mary Todd was one of nine children of Robert Todd, a successful businessman from Lexington, Kentucky. Her close friend when they were growing up in Lexington Kentucky, Margaret Woodrow, described Mary as a young girl:

She was very high strung, nervous, impulsive, excitable, having an emotional temperament much like an April day, sunning all over with laughter one moment, the next crying as though her heart would break.[1]

Mary's father remarried after the death of her mother, and Mary was not at all fond of her step-mother, who felt much the same about her husband Robert's children from his first marriage As a result, the three oldest Todd sisters, Elizabeth, Frances and Mary, all sought to leave home as soon as they could.

A friend of Mary Todd's younger sister, Emily, said that Mary had "clear blue eyes, long lashes, light brown hair with a glint of bronze and a lovely complexion"[2] that was sometimes referred to as peaches and cream. William Herndon described her as "dashing, handsome-witty...cultured-graceful-dignified."[3] She was considered by others as the better-looking and more personable of the three oldest Todd sisters. With ten years of formal education, the last eight of which were at Madame Mentelle's boarding school in her home town of Lexington, Kentucky, Mary was better educated than most of the men and women of her time. She loved to discuss politics and current events, and could do so in French as well as English. At Madam Mentelle's she had also learned all the social skills necessary for a woman who would eventually take her place in marriage beside a successful man. She was an accomplished ballroom dancer, played the piano, and was a master of the art of conversation. Her brother-in-law, Ninian Edwards, said that Mary was so charming that she could cause a bishop to forget his prayers.

Mary probably first heard of Abraham Lincoln from her cousin, John Todd Stuart, who had taken the promising young man as his younger partner at their law firm, Stuart and Lincoln. She did not meet Lincoln until sometime in the fall of 1839, possibly when she attended a political rally in the town square, where Lincoln, Stephen A. Douglas and Edward D. Baker all gave speeches. There is no record of the impression he made on her that day, but he must have piqued her interest.

According to Edwards' family tradition, Mary and Abraham's first face-to-face meeting occurred at a ball at **the Edwards mansion** on Aristocrat Hill. Lincoln awkwardly made his way through a swirling group of dancers and stood beside Mary, shyly stammering out a request for her to dance the next dance with him. She later recalled the meeting, saying that Lincoln told her that he wanted to dance with her in the worst way – and, she punned, that was just what he did.

Courtships in the 1800's followed a well-defined protocol outlined in the social magazines of the day. An unmarried man only called upon an unmarried lady on the invitation of a male member of her household. Any lady who allowed a breach of this protocol was scorned for her "gauche forwardness and spinsterly desperation." Agreements about marriage, even casual verbal ones, were considered as binding as a contract, and often upheld in courts of law with damages awarded to the aggrieved party. Once a man asked for a woman's hand in marriage, she could accept or reject the proposal, or even accept and then change her mind. The courts generally sided with her. Talk of marriage was to be conducted carefully, and only begun when both parties were serious.

Lincoln became a regular visitor to the Edwards household. Mary's sister Elizabeth, who had high hopes for a favorable match for her younger sister, was not thrilled about his attentions to her. She thought him a bad match for her sister. Mary was highly educated; he was self-taught, with less than a year of formal schooling. She spoke French fluently, he spoke with a backwoods twang, often telling off-colored stories offensive to a woman of culture. Mary was five feet tall, barely coming up to the chest of the six-foot four inch Lincoln. It was hard not to smile at the sight of her craning her neck sharply to look up at him. She was gay and spirited, he frequently dark and brooding. Mary's newly married sister Frances weighed in with the opinion that Lincoln was "the plainest man" in Springfield. Elizabeth and Frances feared the match between Lincoln and Mary would end in unhappiness for both of them.

Mary had a wide streak of stubbornness in her, and her family's opposition may have heightened, not lessened, her interest in Abraham Lincoln. She told her cousin Stephen Logan that she saw Lincoln as a "rough diamond" that she could spend her life polishing to shine brighter than any of her other suitors. But despite her attraction to Lincoln, she continued to encourage the attention of her other suitors. Edwin Webb was the most persistent of the lot. A widower with two children, Webb was fifteen years older than Mary. He pressed his suit hard, asking her more than once to marry him. She eventually turned him down, telling her good friend Mercy Levering, "I love him not, and my hand will never be given where my heart is not."[4]

Stephen A. Douglas, a rising star of the Illinois Democratic Party, was also courting Mary. At five foot four and only 90 pounds, Douglas was a brash, intelligent, ambitious politician, whose vast energy belied his small stature. Mary was seen in his company often enough to cause the citizens of Springfield to remember them as "a special couple." Mary claimed later in her life that he did propose to her, and that she rejected his offer of marriage with the words, "I can't consent to be your wife. I shall become Mrs. President, or I am the victim of false prophets, but it will not be as Mrs. Douglas."[5] Some historians believe that Mary was allowing these men to pay her court, not because of any real interest in them on her part, but rather, as a way to kindle the flames of jealousy in Abraham Lincoln, who she felt was far too reticent in his courting of her.

Elizabeth Edwards watched in dismay as Lincoln called on Mary Todd repeatedly, sitting next to her on a black, horsehair settee in the parlor of the Edwards mansion. Elizabeth later recalled that her sister would usually lead the couple's conversation, with Lincoln appearing completely enthralled. "He would listen and gaze on her as if drawn by some superior power."[6]

Abraham and Mary had many differences, but they also had very much in common. They both loved poetry, and could, on a moment's notice, recite whole works of their favorite writers. Both loved to read Shakespeare, and had committed many passages to memory. She was devastated by the loss of her mother at age six. He watched his mother die a painful death at age nine. And, what must also have been fascinating to him about her, she could speak of his political idol (and hers), Kentucky Senator and Whig Presidential candidate Henry Clay, intimately, as he was a good friend of the Todd family, often dining with them at their Lexington home, and bouncing Mary on his knee when she was a child. He had never met such a woman before in his life. And most intoxicating of all to this son of a Kentucky farmer and furniture maker, she seemed attracted to him.

Just as their attraction was beginning to grow into something more, they found themselves separated. In April, 1840 Lincoln had to leave Springfield to ride the Eighth Judicial Circuit, for court was now in session in the rural towns of central Illinois. He was also needed in southern Illinois to make speeches on behalf of Whig candidate for President, William Henry Harrison. And he was standing for re-election to the legislature. With a financial depression hitting the nation hard, Lincoln's expensive internal improvements program was proving to be a hindrance to his re-election.

While he was away, they continued courting by letter. This was probably to Lincoln's benefit, as he always seemed tongue-tied in the presence of young ladies. He would be much more effective communicating his feelings in writing. When he finally returned to Springfield, Lincoln was disappointed to find that Mary had gone off to Missouri to visit with her brother. Their letters continued. Unfortunately, none of those letters to her have ever been discovered, but she did allude to his communications in a letter she sent to a friend in July of 1840:

When I mention some letters I have received since leaving Springfield, you will be somewhat surprised, as I must confess they were entirely unlooked for....[7]

There is speculation that Mary and Lincoln may have come to an agreement during this time, possibly keeping it a secret to avoid the arguments she knew she would hear from her family about how poor a mate Abraham Lincoln was for her.

Then, around or just before New Year's Day, 1841, something happened between Mary Todd and Abraham Lincoln.

***

Just as in the case of Lincoln's relations with Ann Rutledge, there is much divided opinion among historians about what occurred to cause the break-up of Lincoln and Mary Todd.

Elizabeth Edwards told William Herndon in an interview in 1866:

I knew Mr. L. well...he was a cold man – he had no affection – was not social

– was abstracted – thoughtful. L. could not hold a lengthy conversation with a lady – was charmed with Mary's wit and fascinated with her quick sagacity – her will – her nature – and culture...he wanted to marry and doubted his ability and capacity to please and support a wife.[8]

These statements revealed much. Mrs. Edwards's explanation of Lincoln's fears of his inability to support and please a wife echo the exact words he wrote to Mary Owens when he was struggling with his promise to marry her. They also reveal the depth of feeling Elizabeth Edwards and her husband had against Lincoln marrying Mary.

Lincoln probably did have serious doubts about his ability to support Mary and a family, and being a sensitive man, he undoubtedly was painfully aware of Elizabeth and **Ninian Edwards** opposition to the marriage. Ninian and Elizabeth Edwards were her guardians while she lived with them in Springfield, and as a man who placed great importance on doing the honorable thing, he must have been greatly conflicted to be acting against their wishes. But there were more possible reasons for the breakup.

Emily Todd Helm, half-sister of Mary, related another possible reason in a story she told in her book, Mary, Wife of Lincoln. She wrote of a party held sometime around the New Year that Lincoln was to attend with Mary. Lincoln got caught up with some work at the law firm, and arrived late to pick her up. She had grown tired and angry waiting for him, and had already left for the party. When he got to the party, he found her dancing merrily in the arms of his bitter political rival, Stephen

Douglas, laughing and openly flirting with him. Lincoln was enraged and jealous, confronting Mary about it on New Year's Day, 1841. He told her that he would release her from their engagement. She angrily accepted his offer, and with a stamp of her foot said "Go, and never, never come back."⁹

Another possible reason was given by Ninian Edwards and Joshua Speed. Both claimed that Lincoln's resolve to marry Miss Todd was shaken by the realization that he loved another woman, Matilda Edwards. Miss Edwards had come to Springfield in 1840, and was staying at the Edwards mansion, along with Mary, sharing a bed with her. One admirer commented on her willowy figure, and blonde hair that curled "like the wind at play with sunbeams." Mary described Matilda as "a most interesting young lady," who drew "a concourse of beaux & company around us." Ninian Edwards told William Herndon in an 1865 interview that he was certain of Lincoln's attraction to her.

Lincoln fell in love with Miss Edwards...He did not ever by act or deed directly or indirectly hint or speak of it to Miss Edwards. She became aware of this – Lincoln's affections – The Lincoln & Todd engagement was broken off in consequence of it.¹⁰

Lincoln's closest friend, Joshua Speed, in an 1866 interview with Herndon, told a similar story.

Lincoln, seeing another girl & finding he did not love his wife (Mary) wrote a letter saying he did not love her. (Lincoln asked Speed to deliver the letter to Mary, but he refused) Lincoln went to see Mary – told her that he did not love her. She rose – and said – the deceiver shall be deceived, wo is me. Lincoln drew her down on his knee – kissed her – and parted.¹¹

It is difficult to sort through all this and get at the truth. Ninian and Elizabeth Edwards were understandably reluctant in 1866, to admit that they worked hard to discourage Lincoln from marrying Mary. After all, he was now a revered, fallen Savior of the Union, on his way to becoming an icon. So Ninian expanded on a story circulated about in Springfield for years regarding Lincoln's attraction to Matilda Edwards, and gave that as the reason for the broken engagement. His wife Elizabeth claimed that the real reason was that Lincoln feared he could not support Mary properly. Both say nothing of their strong objections voiced to both Mary and Lincoln about their engagement.

I discount Matilda Edwards being the reason for the breaking of the engagement. Mary Todd, who was a passionate, jealous woman by nature, never showed any resentment toward Matilda Edwards after January 1, 1841. They remained on speaking terms well after what Lincoln and others refer to as "the Fatal First." Mary Todd cut people out of her life for much less than stealing a fiancée.

I find the most believable reason for the break-up of the engagement to be found in the Edwards opposition to the marriage, and Lincoln's fear that he could not support Mary in the manner to which she was accustomed. As a man of honor, he could not easily go against the Edwards wishes, and he was still very much in debt from his failures at the grocery business in New Salem. His income as a lawyer was decent, but he could not count on his salary as a legislator, for he had barely been re-elected in August, with his worst finish in his last four attempts. He probably also had doubts about how well he could please a woman of Mary's standing in society, with his humble background, inadequate education and sloppy manner of dress.

Whatever the cause, after January 1, 1841, it became widely known in Springfield that something had happened to end the relationship between Lincoln and Mary Todd. It was Lincoln who showed the effects of this break-up most publicly. He, in an unprecedented display of irresponsibility, missed all the roll call votes in the legislature for the first two weeks of January, even though the Illinois House was in session just blocks from where he was living. On January 17, 1841, Edwin Webb, a member of the Coterie, wrote a letter to Lincoln's friend, Orville H. Browning, describing Lincoln's condition:

Lincoln, you know, was desponding and melancholy when you left. He has grown much worse and is now confined to his bed, sick in body and mind.[12]

James Conkling, another Coterie member, wrote to his soon to be wife (and Mary Todd's closest friend), Mercy Levering, picturing Lincoln as:

...reduced, and emaciated in appearance and seems scarcely to possess strength enough to speak above a whisper.[13]

William Herndon said that Lincoln went "crazy as a loon." Another Springfield citizen gossiped "Lincoln is in a rather bad way...the doctors say he came within an inch of being a perfect lunatic for life."[14] Joshua Speed said that he feared for what Lincoln might do to himself, and removed his razor from their bedroom.

Mary Todd continued to appear in public, seemingly none the worse for the broken affair. Months after the split she wrote to her friend Mercy Levering:

L. deems me unworthy of notice, as I have not seen him in the gay world for months, with the usual comfort of misery, imagine that others were as seldom gladdened by his presence as my humble self, yet, I would the case were different, that 'Richard' should be himself again, much happiness would it afford me.[15]

Sometime in late December 1840 or early January, 1841, despite his deeply troubled state, Lincoln had the presence of mind to consult with a friend and local doctor, **A. G. Henry**. After spending several hours a day with him, Henry diagnosed Lincoln's condition as hypochondriasis. In the medical world of the 19th century this word referred to a disease that was a less severe form of melancholia that could, if not treated, lead to a patient's insanity or suicide. The cause was thought to be black bile that resided in the liver, kidneys, gallbladder, spleen, stomach or intestines.

In the third chapter of a medical book widely in use by physicians of the time, Dr. Benjamin Rush outlined the treatments prescribed to a patient suffering from hypochondriasis. First, the patient would be severely bled, in a procedure involving the cutting of veins, to allow a free flow of blood from the body. This began the process of removing toxins from the body. Second, small, heated glass cups were applied to the patient's body at the temples, behind the ears, and at the nape of the neck. This brought blood up to the surface of the skin, drawing it from the troubled areas. Third, the patient was given purgatives to induce vomiting and diarrhea. These purgatives often included mercury, arsenic and strychnine. This purging would clear the body of any other undesirable fluids that could affect functioning of the vital organs. Then the patient would be kept on a strict diet. This, it was believed, would lead the patient to behave in a less violent manner toward him and others. Once this purging and starving of the body was complete, use of stimulants would be introduced. Sherry or red wine, tea and coffee; ginger and black pepper in large quantity, tar pills in water, garlic or peppermint tea; magnesia, limewater, and milk; and mustard rubs. Quinine might also be administered, along with warm baths to induce sweating, followed by cold baths. [16]

We now know that the purgatives doctors routinely prescribed to induce vomiting are poisonous to the body. Mercury, a key purgative used, also has the side effect of producing depression, anxiety and irritability.

This regimen would wreak havoc on even the strongest of patients. It is not known for certain if Dr. Henry's treatment of Lincoln included any or all these remedies, only that he put him to bed and kept him isolated for two weeks, however, physicians of the time generally used Dr. Rush's approach to curing hypochondriasis. It is no wonder, then, that Lincoln's friends described him in January, 1841 as "emaciated" and "weak," and "crazy as a loon."

Lincoln, perhaps at the urging of his friend Dr. Henry, wrote a letter to Dr. Daniel Drake of Cincinnati, Ohio, describing his condition and seeking further advice on how to deal with it. Dr. Henry considered Dr. Drake to be an expert in the area of melancholy and depression. Joshua Speed related the details he knew of this letter to William Herndon. Herndon never intended to reveal the letter's content, but did so accidentally when he loaned a book of his interview notes to Ward Hill Lamon, who was writing a biography of Lincoln. Lamon subsequently wrote of the letter in his biography.

Speed told Herndon:

Lincoln wrote a letter (a long one which he read to me) to Dr. Drake of Cincinnati descriptive of his case...I think he must have informed Dr. D of his early love for Miss Rutledge – as there was a part of the letter which he would not read.[17]

Herndon, who after Lincoln's death, claimed that Lincoln had spoken to him about his fear that he might have syphilis, had a different belief about what the unrevealed part of Lincoln's letter to Dr. Drake contained:

The note to Dr. Drake in part had reference to his disease and not to his crazy spells, as Speed supposes.[18]

The letter from Lincoln to Dr. Drake has never been found. It is known that Dr. Drake replied to Lincoln saying that he could not recommend treatment without meeting with him. What is also known is that Dr. Drake believed that fresh air and exercise were the best treatments for patients with hypochondria, not isolation and excessive use of purgatives.

Perhaps Dr. Henry and Abraham Lincoln came to that same conclusion. On January 20, 1841 Lincoln finally left his bed and began to appear in public. He wrote to his law partner Congressman John Stuart, in Washington D.C.:

I have, within the last few days, been making a most discreditable exhibition of myself in the way of hypochondriaism...Pardon me for not writing more; I have not sufficient composure to write a long letter.[19]

Three days later he wrote to Stuart again:

For not giving you a general summary of the news you must pardon me, it is not in my power to do so. I am now the most miserable man living. If what I feel were equally distributed to the whole human family, there would not be one cheerful face on the earth. Whether I shall ever be better I can not tell; I awfully forbode I shall not. To remain as I am is impossible; I must die or be better, it appears to me.[20]

By early February, Lincoln's condition seemed to improve. He was able to joke to his partner Stuart in a letter, "You see by this, that I am neither dead nor quite crazy yet."

Adding to Lincoln's agitated state was the fact that his close friend, Joshua Speed, was also struggling through dark times. Matilda Edwards had charmed many of the bachelors of Springfield, but none fell for her harder than Speed and Lincoln. There is testimony to the fact that Lincoln never made this interest known to Matilda because he was already engaged and because he knew his friend Joshua Speed was intent on marrying her. So he allowed Speed to court Matilda, uncontested. Matilda rejected Speed's proposal. She was looking for a man with more property and money than Speed had to offer. He was crushed.

The two men must have been miserable company for each other. Both had always relied on the other to be a sounding board for their plans, hopes and worries. Now, neither could help the other. Speed began complaining to Lincoln and others of "sick headache and the hypo." In March he wrote to his family in Kentucky, "All feeling is dead and dust."

Lincoln was hit hard in April when Speed announced that he was selling his share of the store where they both had been living. He was going home to Kentucky to heal his emotional wounds. Spring of 1841 found Lincoln without his fiancée, his best friend or a place to live.

Darkness once again obscured his future.

***

When the Illinois legislature convened on March 1, 1841, Lincoln's political future appeared bleak. He had barely achieved re-election in his last campaign, and the Democrats were using the continuing financial depression in Illinois to hammer Lincoln, his Whig party and their expensive internal improvements program, as the cause for the state's financial woes. William Henry Harrison's victory in presidential election of 1840 should have been a light of hope for Lincoln, as he had campaigned hard for him across Illinois, but it was not. Illinois Whigs had failed to carry the state for Harrison, and many local offices fell to the Democrats.

In April 1841, John Stuart was busy laying the groundwork for his re-election to Congress, and Lincoln was struggling to regain his emotional balance and political future. They mutually agreed to dissolve their law firm, and Lincoln immediately joined **Stephen T. Logan**, a well-respected Springfield lawyer, as a partner at the new firm of Logan and Lincoln.

Lincoln attempted to use his strong backing of President Harrison to seek a federal appointment. He asked his now former law partner, Congressman John Stuart, to work on his behalf with the President to obtain a posting as charge d' affairs (equivalent to today's post of Ambassador) to New Granada (now called Columbia). This would afford Lincoln an escape from his local political setbacks, the romantic mess he had created with Mary Todd, and it would be consistent with what Dr. Drake espoused as proper treatment for his hypochondriasis

– lots of travel, new surroundings and fresh air.

Stuart's work to obtain the New Granada position for Lincoln ended with President William Henry Harrison's death from pneumonia on April 4, 1841, after only a month in office. His Vice President, John Tyler, a Democrat, assumed the Presidency, effectively ending Lincoln's hopes that he, a Whig, would obtain any federal appointment.

***

After reconsidering his options, Lincoln decided to accept an offer to visit Joshua Speed at his home, Fairview, in Kentucky. After the Illinois legislature adjourned on August 9, he departed for the much needed rest.

For the next several weeks Lincoln enjoyed the company of Speed, his sister and mother at their plantation. It was the grandest home he had ever stayed in, and he found the excellent food and company a balm for his wounded psyche.

Speed had come to Kentucky to heal the emotional wounds he suffered from his failed courtship of Matilda Edwards. When Lincoln arrived at Fairview, instead of finding his friend heartbroken and inconsolable, he discovered that Speed had already fallen under the spell of a lovely neighbor, Fanny Henning. Their courtship progressed over the summer while Lincoln stayed at Fairview.

Back in Springfield, Mary Todd wrote to her friend Mercy Levering, who had left town months before, that she found the hot summer days "too flat, still and unprofitable," and found herself with "lingering regrets over the past."[21]

In September 1841, Lincoln and Joshua Speed departed from Louisville via steamer to journey back to Springfield. Speed was returning to Illinois to close out his business affairs prior to his permanent move to Kentucky.

While Lincoln and Speed were still onboard the steamer making their way to Saint Louis, Mary Todd's close friend, Mercy Levering, married James Conkling, one of the Springfield Coterie. Both Abraham and Mary, upon hearing of the marriage, must have felt that others were moving ahead with their lives while they were still adrift.

Once Lincoln and Speed reached Saint Louis by steamer, they arranged to complete the rest of their journey back to Springfield by carriage, arriving there in mid-September. Speed went about the task of completing the sale of his share of the grocery on the town square, and Lincoln headed out on the judicial circuit, the fall court session having just begun.

On September 27, Lincoln wrote to Joshua Speed's sister, recalling a scene he had witnessed while onboard the steamer carrying him back to Saint Louis. He said he observed a slave master with a coffle of Negroes he was transporting to their new owners, describing them as chained together

...like so many fish upon a trot-line. In this condition they were being separated forever from the scenes of their childhood, their friends, their fathers and mothers, brothers and sisters, and many of them from their wives and children, and going into perpetual slavery where the lash of the master is proverbially more ruthless and unrelenting than any other where.[22]

In a later letter he said, "That sight was a continuous torment to me and I see something like it every time I touch the Ohio."[23]

Whigs around the state were beginning their process of selecting candidates to run for state office in November. Lincoln's name came up as a possible candidate for Governor, but he refused to declare his candidacy, knowing that his damaged reputation as a result of the internal improvements fiasco could hurt Whig chances to secure the office.

***

As winter came and the New Year of 1842 was celebrated, Lincoln was still conflicted about what he considered his bad treatment of Mary Todd the year before. He told Joshua Speed:

There is one still unhappy that I have contributed to make so. That still kills my soul. I cannot but reproach myself, for even wishing to be happy while she is otherwise.[24]

Speed was still worried about his relationship with Fanny Henning, and told Lincoln of his concern about whether being married would live up to his perhaps unrealistic dreams of blissful union. Lincoln wrote to his friend, urging him to ignore reason and let love rule his actions. "Candidly, were not those heavenly black eyes the whole basis of all your early reasoning on the subject?" [25]

On February 15, 1842, **Joshua Speed** married **Fanny Henning** at Fairview, Kentucky. Lincoln was very interested in how his friend would find married life, as both of them had shared their many fears about matrimony and intimacy. He wrote his friend, "Are you now,

in feeling as well as judgement, glad you are married as you are?"
When Speed's response finally came Lincoln tore the letter open with
"intense anxiety and trepidation", and read that Speed was indeed,
finally happy. Lincoln immediately replied:

*I have hardly yet become calm. I feel somewhat jealous of you both now; you
will be so exclusively concerned for one another, that I shall be forgotten
entirely.*[26]

More sadness came Lincoln's way when he heard that his good friend
from New Salem, Bowling Green, had died. It was Green and his wife
who had taken Lincoln in when he was grieving over the death of
Ann Rutledge, and it was Mrs. Green who had been a second mother
to him, darning his socks, mending his trousers, fixing his meals and
trying to get him to speak to her when he seemed alone and lost in
deep sadness. When he tried to give the eulogy over Bowling Green's
grave he broke down and was unable to speak.

***

Lincoln continued to be much in demand as a speaker, despite his loss
of prestige over the failure of Whig programs in the legislature, and
his decision not to stand again for a seat there. On February 22, 1842,
in observance of Washington's Birthday, he was invited to give an
address to the Washington Temperance Society at the Second Baptist
Church in Springfield. What is most notable about the address, which
dealt with the progress being made to halt the scourge of drunkenness
across America, was its resemblance to his earlier speech at the Young
Men's Lyceum in 1838. In his conclusion we hear a repeated theme
about reason, and the first serious comments he makes publicly about
slavery.

*Happy day, when, all appetites controlled, all passions subdued, all matters
subjected, mind, all conquering mind, shall live and move the monarchy of the
world. Glorious consummation! Hail fall of Fury! Reign of Reason, all hail!*

*And when the victory shall be complete-when there shall be neither a slave
nor a drunkard on the earth-how proud the title of that Land, which may*

truly claim to be the birthplace and cradle of both those revolutions, that shall
have ended in that victory. How nobly distinguished that People, who shall
have planted, and nurtured to maturity, both the political and moral freedom
of their species.[27]

Reason over passion is a theme that illuminates a key part of Lincoln's character. His friends often described him as a cold man, who kept his deepest thoughts to himself. Despite his contrary advice to Joshua Speed when encouraging him to marry Fanny Henning, Lincoln's life was a constant struggle to control his passions, and reason out the correct course of action. We see this in how he resolved the dilemma of what he should do about his relationship with Mary Todd.

On March 27, 1842 he wrote to Joshua Speed, "It cannot be told how it now thrills me with joy, to hear you say that you are now far happier than you ever expected to be." He knew how fearful he and Speed were of marriage. Now he had solid evidence that might cause him to reason away that fear.

The next several months found Lincoln travelling outside Springfield to the court houses scattered about the prairies of central Illinois, representing clients and trying cases on the Eighth Judicial Circuit.

Sometime during the summer, friends began working to get Lincoln and Mary Todd to renew their friendship. **Simeon Francis**, Lincoln's friend and editor of the "Sangamo Journal" and his wife, Eliza, thought there could still be a mutual attraction between the couple that might be coaxed into something more. Knowing about the Edwards family's opposition to Lincoln as a partner for Mary, and having been witness to the gossip around town about their break-up, they invited Mary and Lincoln to their home, a place where the estranged couple could meet in private, unknown to the outside world. What was said between the two at their first private meeting in over a year we do not know, but they did continue to meet there, and at the home of Lincoln's friend Dr. A. G Henry, across the rest of the summer. Evidence of their newly re-established closeness is found in a gift that Lincoln presented to Mary Todd that fall. It was a list of election returns from his last three races for the state legislature, wrapped in a pink ribbon. Not the sort of thing that causes a girl's heart to race, but personal and thoughtful, as Lincoln knew Mary's fondness for politics. It was wrapped in a pink ribbon and endorsed to "Molly," his new, more romantic nickname for Mary Todd.

In August, the "Sangamo Journal" published a letter claiming to come from "The Lost Townships," and signed Rebecca. It was a piece of political satire targeted at the egotistical **James Shields**, a Democrat who was currently serving as State Auditor. A second letter had Shields saying to the many ladies about town,

It is distressing, but I cannot marry you all. Too well I know how much you suffer, but do, do remember, it is not my fault that I am so handsome and so interesting.[28]

Soon a third letter appeared in print. Springfield citizens reacted with glee to the well pointed jabs at Shields, and rumors swirled about who had authored the letters. James Shields was enraged to find himself the butt of such well received humor.

By the time a fourth letter appeared in the "Sangamo Journal" it had been discovered that Mary Todd and her best friend **Julia Jayne** (Mary's former best friend Mercy Levering now being married could no longer participate in such girlish activities)

had written the doggerel. This letter was the fictional widow Rebecca's attempt to placate Shield's wounded ego. She offers her hand in marriage to the "rather good lookin than otherwise" Shields:

I know he's a fighting man, and would rather fight than eat, but isn't marrying better than fighting, although it tends to run into it. And I don't think I'd be such a bad match either. I am not over sixty, and am just four foot three in my bare feet, (Shields was short, and sensitive about it) and not much more round the girth.[29]

Mary and Julia were quite pleased with their literary adventure, but Shields, a man of quick and high temper, was publicly embarrassed and livid. He believed Lincoln was the author (Lincoln had, in fact, written the second letter, and parts of the others along with Mary and Julia Jayne), and demanded an apology and retraction. The two exchanged letters, with Lincoln unwilling to reveal Mary and Julia's part in the farce. Shields then lost his patience and insisted on gaining satisfaction by proposing a duel. Lincoln, always careful in matters that involved his honor, did not laugh off the proposal. He appointed Dr. E. H. Merriman as his "second," and asked him to negotiate a settlement with Shields.

Shields refused, and as was the right of the accused party, Lincoln then instructed Merriman to tell Shields that the weapons used would be cavalry broadswords. This was quite an unusual choice, as pistols were most typically used in dueling. Lincoln, standing six foot four, with long arms, could easily wield a long, heavy broadsword and keep the much shorter Shields at bay. Lincoln must have hoped this choice of weapons would give Shields pause to reconsider his challenge, but it did not. Shields was intent on going forward with the duel, regardless of the risk of personal injury. Since dueling was illegal in Illinois, both parties agreed to meet on September 21, 1842, on a small island in the Mississippi River that was in Missouri, where dulling was still legal.

What mixed emotions must Mary Todd have been feeling that day, knowing that Abraham Lincoln was willing to fight a duel to protect her reputation? She had been borne into a world where wounded, aristocratic, southern pride often required dueling to set things straight. Was she proud of him, ashamed of herself for causing such a row, afraid for his life? She could only sit in Springfield and await the outcome.

On September 21, as the mists of early morning still hung low over the Mississippi River, two boats left the shore at Alton, Illinois, and headed out to Blood Island, in the middle of the great river. James Shields and his seconds occupied one craft, Lincoln and his seconds, the other. Once they docked the two groups walked to the center of the small island and began preparations for the event to come. Lincoln, perhaps to intimidate his opponent, picked up his long, heavy broadsword, and slowly extended his arm out straight in front of him, demonstrating his enormous reach, then held the sword steady for some time, showing his strength. Shields paced about in constant motion, alive with nervous energy. As the combatants continued to ready themselves, the seconds for both were hard at work trying to end the whole affair. They quickly reached some sort of agreement, and soon Shields seconds were telling Lincoln's seconds that Shields would withdraw his initial letter of accusation against Lincoln. Lincoln's seconds then read a statement of apology that appears to have already been prepared. As the morning sun burned away the fog blanketing the river, the two parties rowed back to the Alton shore.

How Lincoln really felt about the dueling incident is best illustrated by an event that occurred during the Civil War. A Union soldier approached President Lincoln and Mary during a reception at the White House and asked the President if he had really fought a duel "all for the sake of the lady by your side." Lincoln replied angrily, "I do not deny it, but if you desire my friendship, never mention it again." In a letter written years after the Civil War to a friend, Mary Lincoln said of the duel, "...we mutually agreed never to mention it - except in an occasional light manner between us."[30]

After he returned to Springfield, the clandestine meetings with Mary continued. The public was still unaware of their reconciliation. Then, during an outing to a wedding in Jacksonville, Illinois a week after the duel, their new relationship went public, as both Mary and Lincoln attended, though not as a couple. They were observed together, conversing in a friendly, if not loving manner, and public speculation began again about their future together.

As Lincoln and Mary worked on their relationship, he seemed to be regaining his old humor. A preacher from Cincinnati, Ohio was in Springfield to deliver a sermon on the Second Coming of the Lord. Lincoln was quoted by friends as saying "It is my private opinion that if the Lord has been in Springfield once, he will never come a second time."

In early October Lincoln wrote to Joshua Speed, giving him some details about "the dueling business" that had occurred recently. Then he got to the real reason for writing to his friend. He asked Speed about his marriage:

That you are happier now than you were the day you married her I well know...But I want to ask a closer question – Are you now, in feeling as well as judgement, glad you are married as you are?...Please answer it quickly, as I feel impatient to know.[31]

The reluctant, doubt-filled partner of Mary Todd was trying to make a decision about their future, as soon as possible.

Speed's reply is not known, but it is clear from what followed that Lincoln must have received a reply that gave him reason enough to move ahead and ask Mary Todd for her hand in marriage during that month. They worked out the details at Simeon Francis's home in the days that followed.

On November 3, 1842, Lincoln ran into Ninian Edwards, Mary's guardian, on the street in Springfield. He told Edwards that he had just come from the home of the Reverend Charles Dresser, who had agreed to officiate at his and Mary's wedding that night in Dresser's home. Edwards was shocked and angered, telling Lincoln that his ward would have to be married in the Edwards mansion. It was his right to insist on that. Meanwhile, at the Edwards mansion, Mary told her sister Elizabeth that she was to be wed that night, at Reverend Dresser's. It is probable that the couple had chosen to spring the announcement on Ninian and Elizabeth Edwards in such a manner in order to minimize her relative's opportunity to effectively argue against the match. Elizabeth, quite upset, also argued that her sister should be married at home, and amongst friends. She asked Mary to delay the wedding by one day so that she could prepare food for the celebration, decorate the home properly and send out last minute invitations. Mary agreed to the one day delay, and Lincoln had no objection to it.

On November 4th, Lincoln was at the home of William Butler, dressing for the wedding, when one of Butler's children happened on him, asking where he was going. "To the devil, I suppose", he replied.

The groom arrived at the Edwards mansion, dripping from the cold, hard rain that was falling. Thirty or so guests were gathered there, along with the bridal party. The wedding cakes were still warm, having just come out of the oven. Elizabeth Edwards was not satisfied with them. Everyone knows, she told her husband, that it is bad luck to bake a cake on a Friday. They never turn out well. Mary, in a white satin dress, had three bridesmaids to attend to her. Lincoln had James Matheny as his best man, since Joshua Speed was unable to attend, owing to the short notice. Just how the groom was feeling that day, having finally resolved his inner conflicts over marrying Mary Todd, is unclear. James Matheny said Lincoln looked like he was "going to the slaughter." Mary's sister Francis said that during the ceremony Lincoln was as "cheerful as he had ever been."

Reverend Dresser had to speak loudly to be heard over the din caused by heavy winds driving rain against the windows of the mansion. If anyone in attendance remembered the old adage "Tears for the bride the rain falls on," they did not mention it. When Reverend Dresser came to the end of the vows from the Book of Common Prayers, Lincoln followed his instruction to repeat the words, "With this ring I thee endow with all my goods and chattels, lands and tenements." As he finished, Old Judge Brown, a rough fellow known for always saying what he thought, blurted out in a loud voice "Lord Jesus Christ, God Almighty, Lincoln, the Statute fixes all that." Reverend Dresser fought hard to keep from laughing, regained his composure, and pronounced Abraham Lincoln and Mary Todd man and wife. Lincoln slid a gold band onto Mary's finger. On it were inscribed the words "AL to Mary, Nov 4, 1842, Love Is Eternal."

Chapter Nine

HUSBAND, FATHER, CANDIDATE

After the wedding ceremony the bride and groom dashed out into the cold, wet night, climbed into Abraham's two seater buggy and headed for their new home, the **Globe Tavern**. Mary's sister Frances had stayed there for two years after she married Dr. William Wallace, so Mary was familiar with what her new surroundings would be like. The Globe was once the office of a

stagecoach line. The two story frame building had been improved since those years, but it was still considered only a second- rate hotel, far less elegant than the other major hotel in Springfield, the American House, and quite shabby and drab compared to the stylish Edwards mansion on Aristocrat Hill. The Globe had eight rooms for boarders, served meals at a common table, and offered basic maid and laundry services.

When the excited young couple arrived that night, they headed up to a second floor room and set down their belongings in a room measuring eight by fourteen feet. This small space would be Mary's world for some time to come. The guests living at the Globe were predominately male, and the small lobby area was always crowded and thick with cigar smoke from the male legislators and lobbyists meeting there, loudly discussing the issues of the day. Abraham had a busy schedule, with the Logan-Lincoln law firm working hard to build and service its list of clients. Mary's days were quite different. Her biggest challenge was how to pass the many hours between when her husband left in the morning and when he came home at night.

She was very aware that the ladies magazines and advice books of the day encouraged young married women to immediately immerse themselves in learning to perform the everyday housekeeping tasks that would ensure a successful marriage. One such publication wrote of women who had to live in boarding houses:

Women so situated have nothing to do. Public opinion will not allow her to assist her husband in his business and she cannot interfere in politics.[1]

Mary Lincoln had suffered from severe migraine headaches since her youth, and life at the Globe Tavern could not have helped her condition. There was a small bell tower set atop the hotel, and its bell would ring at all hours, day or night, shaking the whole wooden structure, and rattling its floors, walls and windows when signaling the arrival of stagecoaches. How many times Mary was startled out of a deep sleep by the sharp peal of that bell is not known, but it must have been a major problem. And if the ringing bell did not disturb her sleep, the constant noise associated with guests entering and leaving the hotel all day and night, depending on stagecoach schedules, was certainly an irritant. Finally, there was the sharp crack of hammer on anvil coming from the blacksmith shop right next door to the Tavern, shattering the few quiet moments Mary might otherwise have enjoyed.

Five days after the wedding, Abraham wrote to Sam Marshall, a friend who lived in Shawneetown, Illinois, and talked of several law cases he had been working on. He concluded his letter to Sam with these words:

Nothing new here, except my marrying, which, to me, is a matter of profound wonder.[2]

Lincoln and Mary remained together in Springfield for almost all of November and December, 1843, growing used to each other as all newly marrieds do. He began to realize that she was a light sleeper, frequently startled awake by loud sounds, and that she was deathly afraid of lightning storms. She discovered that he had the unnerving habit of sitting up straight in the bed at night while asleep, speaking unintelligible phrases. Each had to adjust to the other's peculiarities.

They addressed each other in the fashion of the day. Starting with their first meeting, Mary called him Mister Lincoln. After their first child was born, she called him Father. He began their courtship calling her Miss Todd, then Mary, and on rare occasions, Molly, and even more rarely, Puss. Once their first child came, he called her Mother. They took breakfast and dinner at the Globe's common table, with Lincoln, Mary and the other residents of the hotel sharing stories of their daily experiences.

While life for Mary was quite dull at the Globe, Springfield did provide social distractions for the newly married couple. In January, 1843, the town buzzed with excitement about a ball that was to be held honoring the election of Democrat Sidney Breese to the U. S. Senate, and its rumored special guest, Joseph Smith, controversial leader of the Mormon Church. A warrant had just been issued for Smith's arrest, on a charge of murder, with his court appearance to take place the day before the ball. Abraham, the longtime bachelor, must have felt great pride as he walked into that party with Mary on his arm. He knew that her bubbling personality, quick wit, attractive features and stylish dress made her a great asset to him.

***

While Mary struggled to adapt to her new surroundings and ward off boredom, Abraham remained very busy with the heavy work-load at the law firm. During a two month period between December 1842 and the end of January, 1843, he was involved in over 100 different legal actions, including three divorces, eight bankruptcies, and 73 various dispute settlements. He also spent many hours at his desk writing legal documents, among which were papers for an arbitration report, a notice to a client's creditors, and an order for execution of a lien. He was finally making a living and earning a reputation as a reliable lawyer.

In February the Lincoln's attended a party at the Globe Tavern, hosted by General William F. Thornton, for legislators and his friends. A reporter on the scene later wrote about the gathering:

There was a sound of revelry by night, and Springfield's capitol had gathered then, Her beauty and her chivalry bright – The lamps shone o'er fair women and brave men.[3]

For the first time in years, Lincoln in 1843 held no elective office, yet he remained very active politically. William Herndon said of him years later, that his ambition "was a little engine that knew no rest."

On February 8th, Stephen Douglas and several Democrats spoke at the capitol building, arguing in support of President Van Buren's plan to annex the Oregon Territory, which was being claimed by both the United States and England. On the following evening, Lincoln, John J. Hardin and others spoke to outline the Whig position that President

Van Buren's plan was not workable.

Abraham Lincoln was aiming once again to hold elective office. Less than a week after debating the Democrats on the Oregon issue, Lincoln wrote to a former fellow state legislator, Alden Hull, declaring that he wished to be elected to Congress, and asking Hull for his support and help. To another political associate, Richard Thomas, he wrote:

Now if you should hear anyone say that Lincoln don't want to go to Congress...tell him...he is mistaken.[4]

In early March, Lincoln addressed a gathering of Illinois Whigs in the Hall of Representatives in Springfield. He and a few other Whig politicos had been chosen to outline the party's positions favoring a tariff, national bank, distribution of public lands proceeds, and district conventions. His profile as a leader of the Illinois Whig party was growing more and more prominent

The spring session of the 8th judicial circuit was now open, and Lincoln had to leave his wife to fend for herself in Springfield while he headed out to meet with clients of the Logan-Lincoln law firm, and appear for them in cases all around central Illinois. He was away for over a month.

James Conkling wrote to his wife Mercy after having met Lincoln on the circuit in mid-April. He told her he "found Lincoln desperately homesick and turning his head frequently towards the south."[6]

***

In May, 1843 Lincoln wrote to Joshua Speed, giving him all the news about how their friends in Springfield were getting on, and assuring him that all Whigs were unified in their efforts to re-elect John J. Hardin to Congress. He then urged Speed and his new wife to visit Springfield as soon as possible. He would make sure a room was available for them at the Globe Tavern. A probable reason for his strong desire to have Joshua and Fanny visit was the fact that Mary was now pregnant. The visit would be a pleasant diversion for her, and provide her with badly needed female company.

Mary's influence over her husband became apparent when he suddenly began to purchase articles of clothing in May. He had always been a very casual dresser, preferring to wear what was comfortable, regardless of how wrinkled and tattered it might be. The husband of Mary Todd Lincoln now was ordering a new leghorn (straw summer hat), material for a new suit, and a satin stock (collar). He was also going about town in a stovepipe hat (or plug hat), which made him look even taller than he was. In it he would cram all of his important letters and papers, using it like a travelling file cabinet. He had gotten into the habit back in New Salem, when, as postmaster, he apologized to a customer for not being able to locate the man's letters, explaining that he had just gotten a new hat, and must have left the letters in his old one.

Political activity was taking up all of Lincoln's limited free time that summer. The Presidential election campaign of 1844 was starting, and on June 10 Illinois Whigs met in Springfield to choose their electoral ticket. Henry Clay, Lincoln's "beau ideal of a statesman," became their Whig Party choice. Mary was heavily invested in Clay's candidacy as well, since she had known him as a little girl, meeting him many times at her father's home in Kentucky.

Mary Lincoln was struggling through her first pregnancy. Springfield was having a hot summer, and their little room was stuffy and noisy. There were no midwives in the area to assist her, and all of the doctors in Springfield were male. Her best friend Mercy Levering Conkling was not living in the area, and Lincoln was either away on the circuit, or coming home late each night, exhausted from a full workload of legal work during the day, followed by evenings of political meetings.

Lincoln wrote that summer to Joshua Speed:

We shall look with impatience for your visit this fall. Your Fanny cannot be more anxious to see my Molly(Mrs. Lincoln) than the latter is to see her, nor so much as I am – Don't fail to come – We are but two, as yet.

On August 1, 1843, Mary gave birth to their first child, a boy she named (custom called for the wife to name the first child) **Robert Todd Lincoln,** after her father. The delivery was apparently without incident, as there is no mention of the mother or infant having suffered any unusual difficulties. Robert was healthy, with the single exception that his left eye was slightly crossed. This would lead, during his childhood, to him being teased by his playmates and called "Cockeye."[7]

It was customary for the new mother to remain in bed for up to two months, assisted in caring for the newborn by a nursemaid or relatives. Mary's family was not a source of help. She could not abide being in the same room as her step-mother, and her sister Elizabeth had recently given birth herself. Her husband, distracted as he was by work and politics, was probably not available as much as she would have liked. When Robert was only six weeks old, Lincoln headed off on the circuit, and would remain away much of the time until October. Lincoln's travels on the judicial circuit took up three months in the spring of every year, and three in the fall. Mary managed this difficult time with the help of a fellow boarder, Mrs. Alfred Bledsoe, who bathed and fed baby Robert, giving Mary precious time to recuperate. Mrs. Bledsoe's daughter, who also pitched in when necessary, later wrote of that time:

I was very fond of babies and took on myself the post of amateur nurse...I remember well how I used to lug this rather large baby about to my great delight... [8]

In the early fall, the Lincoln's left the Globe Tavern and moved to a small, three room cottage at **214 South Fourth Street** in Springfield. It was a rental, for which they paid $100 per year. Abraham and Mary finally had a home of their own, where she could cook and clean and tend to baby Robert without the distracting din of noise that always surrounded them at the Globe.

By December of 1843 the Presidential election campaign was in full swing, with Lincoln travelling across the state speaking on behalf of Henry Clay for President. He was chosen that month by his party as one of nine Presidential electors, who would cast their Electoral College ballots for Clay, should he win Illinois' popular vote.

Just before Christmas 1843, Mary's father, Robert Todd came to town to meet his new grandson and namesake. He very generously gifted Mary $25 in gold, an eighty acres parcel of land southwest of the city, and an annuity of $125 to continue until his death. He also gave his son-in-law Abraham approval to begin legal action to collect a debt owed to him. He told the couple that if Lincoln was successful in collecting the debt, they could keep the money. This newfound income allowed Abraham and Mary to begin planning to purchase a permanent home for their family.

***

There is general agreement amongst historians that in 1842, Abraham Lincoln, Edward Baker and **John J. Hardin**, all of whom wished to run for Congress, had reached an agreement. Each would run in turn and serve one term, with Hardin going first, followed by Baker, then Lincoln. That way, Whig party unity would be insured, and since the 7th district was heavily Whig in voting preference, they would be elected over any Democrat. Unity, and strength derived from it, was the key. With that strategy in effect, Hardin won a seat in Congress for the 1842-1844 term.

In early 1844 political infighting amongst Illinois Whigs was intense, as **Edward Baker** and Abraham Lincoln maneuvered to gain their party's nomination as the Whig candidate for a seat in Congress from the 7th district in 1844, to replace John J. Hardin, the Whig who currently held the seat.

One of the main Democratic newspapers in the state, the "Springfield Register" reported in their March 17th edition,

Our ears are stunned here, just now, by the din of the Whigs concerning Lincoln and Baker, as to which shall go to

Congress from this district...Next Monday the Whigs of Sangamon County are to make their choice...Whichever is defeated is to withdraw.[5]

In May, 1844, the state Whigs met in convention at Tremont Illinois, and despite their conflicting ambitions, Lincoln and Hardin withdrew their candidacies so that Edward Baker could take his turn as the Whig candidate for Congress from Illinois' 7th district. After the convention, Lincoln remarked that he felt like "a fellow who is made groomsman to the man who had cut him out, and is marrying his own dear gal."[9]

David Davis, an attorney who travelled the 8th Circuit with Lincoln wrote that spring:

Politics rage now hereabouts...The first day of every court is occupied with political speaking, usually by an Elector on each side of politics, each person generally taking some three or four hours...Lincoln is the best stump speaker in the state.[10]

Campaigning for Whig Henry Clay for President and Edward Baker for Congress continued through the spring and summer, with Lincoln speaking at any courthouse green where a handful of voters could be gathered to listen. Stephen Douglas often appeared at the same locations as one of the spokesmen for the Democratic Presidential candidate, James K. Polk.

In early December, Stephen Logan and Abraham Lincoln amicably ended their partnership in the Logan-Lincoln law firm. Lincoln was now well established as a member of the legal community in Illinois, and he was ready to form a law firm of his own. William Herndon,

the son of a friend from New Salem days, had just been admitted to the bar, and Lincoln offered him a position as his partner. Herndon was flattered to accept the offer, and soon they hung a shingle reading Lincoln and **Herndon**, Attorneys at Law, outside their office located on the second floor of a retail business, directly across the street from the state capitol building.

With the contest for the Whig nomination for Congress from the 7th district done, and having hammered out with his competitors a plan to run for Congress in two years, Lincoln took time to make yet another move with his young family. They left their rented cottage and moved into the first and only home they would ever own, a one and a half story frame house at the intersection of Eighth Street and Jackson, in Springfield. It was painted a pale chocolate brown, with shutters of deep green. The Lincoln's had purchased it from the Reverend Charles Dresser, the Episcopal minister who married them two years before. It was a modest home in a good, but not fashionable neighborhood of Springfield.

At age 35, Abraham Lincoln had a wife and child, a flourishing law career and a bright political future that seemed to point to a seat in the U. S. House of Representatives. Periods of gloom still overtook him, but with less frequency, and seemed to pass quickly.

Mary now had help in getting chores done around the home. There is a recording in a business ledger from one of the stores in Springfield showing that on September 30, the Lincoln's "hired girl" made a purchase of cambric, a plain, white weave linen cloth. She was still a long way from the kind of life she enjoyed at her father's large, brick home in Kentucky, with multiple servants and nanny's to fulfill her every need, but Mary and her husband were beginning to **enjoy a life with some comforts.**

The Whig party of Indiana, knowing Lincoln's reputation as a speaker, asked him to campaign there on behalf of Henry Clay for President. They felt that with his ties to Indiana as a young man, and all the friendships he had formed there, he could be influential in bringing more Whig voters to the polls. So, in October of 1844, Lincoln returned to the southern Indiana lands where his mother, sister, aunt and uncle were buried. He gave a speech in Gentryville, late in the month, defending Henry Clay's position favoring a high protective tariff. Josiah Crawford, his old employer at the local grocery, was sitting in the front row, beaming with pride at how far his clerk had come in the world. A few days later, according to Nathaniel Grigsby, a former schoolmate, Lincoln gave another speech in Carlin Township, about ¾ of a mile from where the cabin his father had built still stood.

Lincoln was deeply moved by this homecoming, but he said little about it at the time. A year later he wrote two poems about his life in Indiana as a boy, and of his feelings on seeing his old home again. We will examine these writings and what they revealed of his thoughts and temperament later.

By late December 1844, votes around the country had been counted and tallied up, and Lincoln and his Whig party learned that Democrat James K. Polk had defeated Henry Clay for the Presidency. This was more than a political loss for Abraham Lincoln. Clay had been his political idol since childhood, and his rejection must have seemed like a rejection by the country of Lincoln's own ideals. Despite the positive news that Edward Baker had succeeded in retaining the seat in Congress formerly held by John J. Hardin for the Whig party, Lincoln remained in a very dark mood for a week after the election results came in.

The social whirl of the state capitol allowed Lincoln no prolonged mourning for Clay's defeat. The turning of the New Year meant parties, and the Lincoln's attended several. On New Year's Day there was "a large and very general party at the state house... the night was one of great hilarity and enjoyment."[11] Two days later they were amongst over 400 guests at the Edwards mansion, Mary Lincoln's sister's home, for a holiday soiree.

***

The early months of 1845 found Lincoln devoting himself to his work at the Lincoln-Herndon law offices, and mixing in a healthy amount of political activity. He joined a group of Springfield Whigs and Democrats who met every Monday evening to provide themselves with entertainment through informal debates on all the local and national issues of the day.

He spent time helping his friend James Conkling achieve success in an election for mayor of Springfield. This was an election that Mary must have followed closely, as Conkling was a former member of the Coterie who had married Mary's close friend Mercy Levering.

He and Mary also spent hours together at night discussing Lincoln's next personal goal, election to the U.S. House of Representatives. He had set his sights on it back in 1842, and had patiently waited for his turn to come, per the agreement he had reached back then with the other two highly ambitious Whigs who sought the same 7th district seat, John Hardin and Edward Baker. Both of them had run for the seat and won it with Lincoln's help. Now he expected them to help him in the contest that was to begin in the spring. As was his style, he and Mary worked up extensive lists of prominent men in each area of the district, who he would solicit for support, and studied in detail election results in each of the last several Congressional elections. Lincoln was not a man to leave anything to chance that he could carefully plan for.

The fall season of the 8th Circuit Court opened in September, and Lincoln travelled to its several courthouses to meet his clients and try their cases. This allowed him to meet key local political figures in those communities and gather their pledges of support for his bid for Congress. He also utilized the lists he and Mary had compiled to begin a letter writing campaign. On September 13 he wrote to Williamson Durley:

When I saw you at home, it was agreed that I should write you and your brother Madison...I was glad to hear you say that you intend to bring about, at the next election in Putnam, a union of the Whigs proper.[12]

In this letter Lincoln began to make public his stand on two issue that would loom large not only in Illinois, but around the nation in the months to come; the annexation of the Republic of Texas into the Union, and slavery.

I never was much interested in the Texas question. I never could see much good to come of annexation...I think annexation an evil. I hold it to be a paramount duty of us in the free states, due to the union of the states, and perhaps to liberty itself,(paradox though it may seem) to let the slavery of the other states alone; while, on the other hand, I hold it to be equally clear that we should never knowingly lend ourselves directly or indirectly, to prevent that slavery from dying a natural death-to find new places for it to live in, when it can no longer exist in the old.[13]

The position that Lincoln took in this 1844 letter is almost exactly the same position he found himself espousing in his run for the White House sixteen years later. That is remarkable when you consider today's politicians, who seem to trim their sails to catch the prevailing winds of popular opinion with disturbing ease.

Lincoln had been hearing rumors that, despite their agreement to "rotate" the 7th district Congressional seat between himself, Edward Baker and John J. Hardin, the latter was acting like he might yet contest Lincoln for the Whig nomination. In an attempt to stop Hardin from running against him, Lincoln began to work on a strategy of deflection. He wrote letters to encourage fellow Whigs to come out in support of Hardin for Governor, hoping that this would interest Hardin enough to "jiggle him" out of running for one office in favor of another.

With the cold and snows of winter closing out his options to travel the district campaigning, Lincoln continued to write a steady stream of letters to all of his friends, instructing them about who in their own communities to talk to, and what to say in his behalf. A December letter to B. F. James reveals how Lincoln's strategy against Hardin had continued to evolve:

...let nothing be said against Hardin. ..Let the pith of the whole argument be 'Turnabout is fair play.'[14]

Throughout December 1844 and January, 1845, Lincoln's surrogates in the 7th Congressional district kept up a steady stream of speeches, letters and newspaper articles endorsing Lincoln for Congress. In February, B. F. James had an article published in his local paper, the Tazewell Whig that typified these efforts:

We conceive it due to Mr. Lincoln, that the people of this district should pay a substantial tribute to his worth, energy and patriotic exertions in behalf of Whig principles.[15]

By February 16th, John J. Hardin had seen and heard enough from Lincoln and his campaign. He wrote and published a public letter declining to be a candidate for Congress. Lincoln's path to the Whig nomination for Congress, and almost certain election to it, was clear of all serious obstacles.

The stresses on Abraham Lincoln were beginning to grow during his campaign for Congress. Long hours working on court cases were followed by long hours writing letters to campaign surrogates and supporters. Food on the judicial circuit was sketchy at best, sometimes inedible. And his sleep must have been uneasy as he contemplated how his wife was coping with their new baby at home without his help. Stress frequently brings on depression, and it was at this time that Lincoln began to fixate on death.

He had for some time been exchanging bits of poetry with a friend, Andrew Johnston, a lawyer from Quincy, Illinois. On February 24th Lincoln sent Johnston a copy of a poem he was very fond of, called *Mortality*. He had read it so many times that he could recite it from memory, and over the remaining years of his life would do just that for countless people. The poem begins:

Oh! Why should the spirit of mortal be proud!

Like a swift, fleeting meteor-a fast-flying cloud –

A flash of lightning – a break of the wave –

He passeth from life to his rest in the grave.

The leaves of the oak and the willow shall fade,

Be scattered around and together be laid;

And the young and the old, and the low and the high

Shall molder to dust and together shall lie.

After several more equally grim stanzas, the poem concludes:

Tis the wink of an eye, tis the draught of a breath,

From the blossoms of health, to the paleness of death.

From the gilded saloon, to the bier and the shroud

Oh, why should the spirit of mortal be proud! [16]

That Lincoln so loved this piece reveals the darkness and fatalism that ran just below the surface of his public character.

In the same letter to Andrew Johnston, which contained a copy of William Knox's poem *Mortality*, Lincoln mentioned a poem of his own that he was working to complete. "I have a piece that is almost done, but I find a deal of trouble to finish it." Since the year before, when he had toured the Indiana area where his family cleared virgin forest, erected a simple cabin, and suffered the tribulations of frontier life for a dozen years, he had been trying to express in poetry, all the emotions that experience had churned up. He enclosed the first ten stanzas of his attempt for Johnston to read, explaining that he was not yet satisfied with it.

It began:

My childhood's home I see again,

And gladden with the view;

And still, as memory crowds my brain,

There's sadness in it too.

O Memory! Thou midway world

Twix't earth and paradise,

Where things decayed and loved ones lost

In dreamy shadows rise.

The first ten stanzas conclude:

I hear the loved survivors tell

How naught from death could save,

Till every sound appears a knell,

And every spot a grave.

I range the field with pensive tread,

And pace the hollow rooms,

And feel (companion of the dead)

I'm living in the tombs.[17]

Gloom almost drips from the pages of this work. Yet Abraham Lincoln never yielded fully to this powerful force of negativity in his character. We will examine in the final chapter of this book how he fought to keep this darker side of his nature from overwhelming him.

Sometimes happy events shocked him out of his melancholy. On March 10, 1846, just such an event occurred, with the birth of his second child, a boy. He and Mary named their second son Edward Baker Lincoln, after a political competitor who both parents now considered a friend. Lincoln wrote to Joshua Speed that Eddie was "rather of a longer order" than Robert, who bore more of the Todd family physical traits. The baby brought much joy to the growing Lincoln household, but he brought concern as well. He seemed more inclined to sickness that his older brother.

One month after Eddie's birth Lincoln again headed out on the spring judicial circuit for months, leaving Mary to cope with a newborn and a three year old as best she could.

The Whigs of the 7th Congressional district met on May 2, 1846 and formally endorsed Abraham Lincoln as their candidate for the U. S. House of Representatives. It only remained for Lincoln to wage an aggressive fall campaign and this naturally Whig district would award him his dream of the past six years, a place on the national stage, in Washington D. C.

Lincoln's district, along with the rest of America, was raging with war fever. Mexico and the U. S. had been arguing over ownership of a small strip of land along the Rio Grande River that separated Mexico from Texas. President Polk had tried to end the difficulty by offering to buy the area from Mexico, but Mexican President Santa Anna refused to sell. Polk then ordered a small garrison of U. S. troops to camp out on an island in the middle of the Rio Grande River, in the disputed area. Their orders were to camp there and await developments. If Polk was gambling that Santa Anna would not tolerate this encroachment into what the Mexican President believed was his territory, and would therefore be provoked into action, he was correct. Mexican forces fired on the camp, and President Polk asked Congress to declare the United States to be at war with Mexico, claiming that U. S. troops were on American soil when fired upon. An army under General Zachary Taylor, which President Polk had earlier ordered to the border, was ordered to move into northern Mexico.

This issue put Lincoln in a tough position. He had opposed the annexation of the Republic of Texas into the Union, fearing extension of slavery. Now there was a possibility that not only would Texas be open to slavery, but any part of Mexico that might be seized as well. Popular sentiment was so strong against Mexico and for the war that he had to carefully calibrate his statements so that he would not ruin his chance at gaining a seat in Congress. Even many Whigs were succumbing to the patriotic lure of glory in battle. Former Whig Congressman John J. Hardin began to recruit men to form the First Illinois Volunteer Infantry Regiment, of which he would be Colonel. In December, Edward Baker, for whom the Lincoln's had named their son Eddie, resigned his seat in Congress (he was to yield it to Lincoln soon anyway) to recruit and command the Fourth Illinois Volunteer Infantry Regiment. The march to war had begun.

The fall campaign found Lincoln running as a Whig against **Reverend Peter Cartwright**, a travelling minister of the fire and brimstone variety. Cartwright was widely known and well liked, and the battle was a tough one. The roughest patch came when Cartwright and his supporters began to print up circulars characterizing Lincoln as a friend to drunkards (citing his association with many reformed drinkers in the Temperance Society), and a hater of Jesus Christ. They called him an infidel, and brought up the rumors about a pamphlet that Lincoln had written which attacked the Bible and organized religion. Fearing the charges might shake loose some of his support Lincoln wrote and published a handbill that answered the charges. He addressed it "To the Voters of the Seventh Congressional District":

Fellow Citizens,

A charge has gotten into circulation in some of the neighborhoods of this district, in substance that I am an open scoffer at Christianity...That I am not a member of any Christian Church is true, but I have never denied the truth of the Scriptures and I have never spoken with intentional disrespect of religion in general.

I do not think I could myself be brought to support a man for office whom I know to be an open enemy of, and scoffer at, religion. Leaving the higher matter of eternal consequence between him and his maker, I still do not think any man has the right to thus insult the feelings, and injure the morals, of a community in which he may live. If then, I was guilty of such conduct, I should blame no man who would condemn me for it; but I do blame those, whoever they may be, who falsely put such a charge in circulation against me.[18]

Voters weighed the charges by Cartwright against Lincoln's refutation, and rewarded Lincoln with victory in the election. On August 3, 1846, Abraham Lincoln received 6, 340 votes, Peter Cartwright, 4, 829. The one-time field hand and self-educated lawyer was now a Congressman-elect.

You would think that after achieving this long sought goal, Abraham Lincoln would bask in some moments of self-congratulation and celebration. Instead, he took time to complete the second canto of the poem he was writing about his return to his former home to Indiana. In it, he focused on the sad tale he had learned on that trip, about a former childhood friend, Matthew Gentry, who had suffered some sort of mental breakdown, and was now a rambling, incoherent shell of his former self.

But here's an object more of dread

Than ought the grave contains –

A human form with reason fled,

While wretched life remains.

He concluded the poem, seemingly fascinated with the specter of death.

O death! Thou awe inspiring prince,

That keepst the world in fear,

Why dost thou tear more blest ones hence,

And leave him ling'ring here? [19]

Death seems to have always been in Lincoln's thoughts, even at the happiest of times.

***

Mary began to prepare the family for the move to Washington D.C. They would not depart for several months, but there was much to do. Lincoln continued to work with his firm's clients and began to prepare William Herndon to take over the full work-load of the firm when he departed to take up his seat in Congress.

In October, Lincoln wrote to Joshua Speed. He described his two young sons to his friend, and confessed "Being elected to Congress...has not pleased me as much as I expected."

There were probably several reasons for this feeling of disappointment. One might have come from Lincoln's realization that because of the "rotation" system he had agreed to with fellow Whigs in the 7th district, he would only have one two-year term in Congress to make his mark before yielding his seat to another. His sadness might also have been caused by the fact that despite Lincoln's 1846 Congressional victory, Democrats had swept most other offices in the state, and gained control of the Illinois House. And last, he may have felt that his success had been eclipsed by Democrat **Stephen A. Douglas**. In December 1846, the Democrats, now in control of the state legislature, voted Douglas into the U. S. Senate. His old adversary always seemed to be one step ahead of him.

The war with Mexico was raging as the New Year of 1847 approached. U.S. troops under Zachary Taylor's army moved south into Mexico and Mexican President Santa Anna moved his army north to oppose it. On February 23, 1847, Col. John J. Hardin was killed during the battle of Buena Vista. There was much history between Lincoln and

Hardin, and the death of this ambitious, talented man must have shocked him.

July found Abraham Lincoln visiting the growing metropolis of Chicago, as a member of the Sangamon County delegation sent to the Harbor and Rivers Convention convened there. One of the attendees, Elihu Washburn of Galena, Illinois, saw Lincoln strolling down the street near his hotel and said to his friends:

There is Lincoln on the other side of the street. Just look at Old Abe. And from that time we all called him Old Abe. No one who saw him can forget his personal appearance at the time. Tall, angular, and awkward, he had on a short-waisted, thin, swallow tail coat, a short vest of the same material, thin pantaloons, scarcely coming to his ankles, a straw hat, and a pair of brogans with woolen socks.[20]

Away from home and his wife, Lincoln was not making the kind of sartorial impression she hoped he would. Had she been with him, he probably would have been better dressed.

In October Lincoln became involved in a case involving a runaway slave and his family. Anthony Bryant and his family had escaped from their master, Robert Mason, and fled his Kentucky plantation for Illinois. Once they arrived in the free state of Illinois, they were apprehended and locked up in a Charleston, Illinois jail. Attorneys for the slave family asked Abraham Lincoln to help them secure the family's freedom, but Lincoln turned them down, as he had already agreed to represent the slave owner. The judge ordered the family discharged from the sheriff's custody and from "all servitude whatever from henceforth and forever." As a lawyer, Lincoln believed that everyone deserved representation before the law, but it is doubtful that he was too upset about losing this case.

With that case finished, the Lincoln family completed preparations to depart Springfield for Washington D. C. They rented out their home on Eighth Street for one year, for the price of $90. On October 25th they began their trip by travelling to Saint Louis, where they met up with Joshua Speed. Speed joined them for the next part of their journey, to Lexington, Kentucky, where the Lincoln's would briefly visit with Mary's father and step-mother, before continuing on to Washington D. C.

The "Illinois Journal" (formerly known as the "Sangamo Journal"), reported on their trip:

Mr. Lincoln, the member of Congress elect from this district, has just set out on his way to the city of Washington. His family is with him; they intend to visit their friends and relatives in Kentucky before they take up the line of march for the seat of government. He will find many men in Congress who possess twice the good looks, and not half the good sense, of our own representative. [21]

The family arrived in Lexington, Kentucky on November 2, and remained there until November 25, 1847. During their stay, Lincoln attended a speech given by his political idol, Henry Clay. Clay spoke about the Mexican War, denouncing it as a war of aggression by the United States. This position taken by Clay undoubtedly influenced Lincoln's thoughts, as he considered how he would handle this difficult issue in the upcoming session of Congress.

Lincoln and his family arrived by train in Washington D. C. on December 2. They checked into Brown's Hotel for the night, and then moved the next day to **Mrs. Spriggs boarding house**, where many

members stayed when Congress was in session. It would be Lincoln's residence for the next two years.

It had been a very long road from his family's log cabin in Kentucky to the nation's Capital.

William Kolasinski

Chapter Ten

CONGRESSMAN LINCOLN

When the Lincoln's moved to the nation's capital in 1847, they faced substantial changes in their lifestyle. Washington D.C. was a city nearly ten times the size of Springfield, Illinois. As a Congressman, Abraham Lincoln would be earning less money than he had as a successful lawyer, so the family's budget would have to be carefully managed. This presented a real challenge in a city where members of Congress were expected to entertain, and their wives were judged by the quality of the fashions they wore. Mary Lincoln took pride in her ability to sew and make her own dresses and clothes for her children, and in Springfield, that clothing was up to middle class standards. In Washington D.C., no matter how well she sewed them, her dresses would be seen as dowdy and plain. There would be stresses and difficulties, but the Lincolns were prepared to meet them together. Mary believed that their time in Washington D. C. would be a fitting reward for her having survived as housewife raising her young boys nearly alone while her husband was away pursuing office.

The city itself was a study in contrasts. Pigs roamed in the streets, with their droppings soiling the hems of ladies' Parisian outfits as they carefully crossed the boulevards. Dilapidated slave pens, filled with hundreds of Africans awaiting sale to new masters, were located within sight of the magnificent marble edifice of the Capitol buildings. In the taverns and stores, churches and houses of ill-repute, soft southern accents mingled with the nasal twang of New Englanders.

In Congress, John C. Calhoun and Jefferson Davis spoke powerfully in the U. S. Senate in defense of slavery and States rights, while Daniel Webster and Henry Clay argued for internal improvements and a strong central government. Democrats in Congress defended their President, James K. Polk, and the war with Mexico that had begun under his administration, while Whigs attacked Polk for provoking a war without Congressional approval.

On December 6, 1847, **Abraham Lincoln** took his seat in the United States House of Representatives, a junior member of a 200 person deliberative body that would wrestle with some very serious national issues during the next two years. Over the House Speaker's chair, a large clock with a yellowed face read 12 noon, and above the clock a statue stared down on the house members. It was a sculpted female figure representing History, and she was there to remind all who saw her that she would be judging their actions.[1]

***

While her husband was at work, Mary Lincoln struggled to adapt to her new surroundings. The Spriggs boarding house was a two story wooden structure situated one street away from the capitol building, which gave her husband a very short walk to work. It was not typical in those days for a Congressman to have his family live with him in Washington. A Congressman's work hours were long and unpredictable, making a regular domestic life difficult, but Mary and Abraham wanted to share this adventure, so she did what she needed to do to make it work.

Mary had the additional burden of having two young children to care for, four-year-old Robert and eighteen-month-old Eddie. They would all be living in a cramped apartment, quite a step down from the comfortable home they owned on Eighth Street in Springfield, Illinois. Mary would no longer have a servant to assist her, or relatives and neighbors to converse with. The clientele of Mrs. Spriggs boarding house was overwhelmingly male. She had her hands full, keeping control of Robert as he ran up and down the halls and stairs, exploring the boarding house, while little Eddie cried for attention.

***

His position as a U. S. Representative would give Abraham Lincoln a chance to grow beyond the parochial concerns of central Illinois. He would now have a say in how the government managed its $60 million dollar budget. He was assigned to membership on the two House committees; one on post offices and the other on War Department expenditures. His Whig Party held a voting majority in the House, with the Democrats holding a similar majority in the U.S. Senate.

The Mexican War, which had been going on for almost two years, was at the center of much of the debate in both houses of Congress. American armies had been successful in driving Mexican forces led by their President, Antonio Lopez De Santa Anna, back from the Texas border toward their capital in Mexico City. Victory seemed inevitable, but it was coming at a cost. $27million dollars had been spent to raise, train, equip, transport and supply American troops. Over 27,000 American soldiers had lost their lives. As the end of conflict approached, arguments in Congress began about whether the

U. S. should permanently occupy the lands it had conquered, eventually annexing them, and if so, whether to continue Mexico's policy against the institution of slavery, or allow these new lands to be opened to the expansion of slavery. Southern Whigs and Democrats tended to vote as a block in favor of slavery. Northern representatives, regardless of party, tended to vote together against the spread of the institution to new lands.

Many Whigs in Congress opposed President Polk's reasons for beginning the conflict. They insisted that President Polk had started the war to open new lands up for slave expansion. Only months after the conflict began, Representative David Wilmot of Pennsylvania attempted to tack a proviso onto a bill before Congress. The proviso proposed that slavery be banned from any lands acquired by the United States as a result of the war with Mexico. This Proviso stirred up Congress' low burning passions over slavery until they grew into red hot debate. Before his election to Congress, Lincoln held the opinion that President Polk had manipulated the U.S. into an unnecessary conflict, and as a new Representative, he continued to hold that belief. It was a risky position to take, for support for the war was strong in his Illinois district. Lincoln attempted to soften his constituent's anger with him by continually voting for all bills that provided support for the troops in the field, but despite that, damage was being done to his reputation at home.

On December 20, 1847, just weeks after taking his oath of office as a new Congressman, Lincoln voted against a resolution declaring the war just and necessary. Two days later he rose in the House of Representatives to offer a resolution calling on the President to inform the House whether "the spot" on which American blood was first shed in the Mexican War was within territory claimed by Mexico. He was certain that it was.

Three weeks later Lincoln again rose from his seat in the house to attack Democratic President Polk's war policy, and defend his Spot Resolution. "The President is, in no wise, satisfied with his own positions...He is a bewildered, confounded, and miserably perplexed man."[2]

Back home in Illinois, voters were not pleased with their new representative's opposition to the war. On January 31, 1848, Lincoln's law partner wrote to him, questioning his stand on the issue, telling him that he was now being derided as "Spotty" Lincoln. Lincoln replied to Herndon saying "I will stake my life, that if you had been in my place, you would have voted just as I did." Herndon answered Lincoln's letter with yet another defense of President Polk and the war. If Lincoln had any doubts about the risky position he had taken, he did not show it. He sent off a reply to Herndon:

Allow the President to invade a neighboring nation whenever he shall deem it necessary to repel an invasion and you allow him to... make war at pleasure. Your view...places our President where Kings have always stood.[3]

***

Lincoln was finding his time Congress a challenge, but he was still able to find some joy in his time in Washington. He and Mary spent one evening attending a performance of "the Ethiopian Serenaders" at Carusi's saloon. A fellow resident at Mrs. Sprigg's boarding house recalled "scenes of merriment" when Lincoln, seated alongside Mary at the communal dining table, would regale everyone with his stories and jokes. Lincoln found other ways to relieve the stress of political debates. On some days he would stop at Caspari's bowling alley on his way home, to play a game of ten-pin with fellow Whig Congressmen. On other occasions he would pull up a chair near the fireplace in the House of Representatives post office and tell tales of New Salem and the woods of Kentucky. A newspaper man said "By New Year's he was recognized as the champion storyteller of the Capitol."[4]

Mary Lincoln did not find her time in Washington as rewarding as her husband. She was exhausted by constantly having to corral her rambunctious two and five year olds, and frustrated with having to hear the complaints of other residents about the noise they created.

She could not entertain callers at her crowded little apartment, and had little funds to dress appropriately for soirees she received invitations to, such as those hosted by Dolly Madison, a former First Lady, whose husband President James Madison, was one of Mary's relatives. She also felt that her husband believed her presence was a distraction that kept him from the performance of his duties in Congress. Exactly what caused her to leave is not known, but in late February, 1848, after only three months in Washington D. C., **Mary** packed up her two children and departed the capitol for her father's home in Lexington Kentucky.

Part of the reason for her departure may be surmised from a letter Lincoln wrote her soon after she and the children left.

All in the house – or rather all with whom you were on decided good terms – send their love to you. The rest say nothing.[5]

***

The war with Mexico was almost at an end. General Winfield Scott had marched an army from Vera Cruz on the Gulf of Mexico, across hundreds of miles, and laid siege to Mexico City. President Santa Anna met with U. S. diplomats and hammered out the treaty of Guadalupe Hidalgo, which awarded large areas of Mexican provinces to the United States (those areas include what are today the states of California, Arizona and New Mexico). The treaty was forwarded to Washington, and the Senate voted to approve and accept it on March 10, 1848. Most citizens of the United States applauded President Polk for waging and winning the war. Abraham Lincoln was on record numerous times in opposition to it.

The attentions of the members of Congress moved swiftly from debate over the status of slavery in newly acquired lands to the upcoming Presidential election. In May, Democrats met in Baltimore and nominated Lewis Cass, a Michigan senator, as their candidate for President, and Millard Fillmore, a local New York politico, as his Vice Presidential running mate.

Whigs were nervous about this election. Many had gone on record against the war, now viewed favorably by much of the nation's citizens. How could they neutralize the negative opinion voters might have of them? They came up with the answer at their convention, held in Philadelphia a month later. After four ballots, they selected an early hero of the war, General Zachary Taylor, who had won stirring victories as Buena Vista and Monterrey. Taylor was a professional soldier and Southern plantation owner from Louisiana who had not taken a public position on expansion of slavery into new territories.

Lincoln had been pushing for Taylor's nomination for months, and was immediately tapped by his party to be an elector for Taylor representing Sangamon County. As such, he was expected to campaign vigorously for Taylor in Illinois in the months to come.

Though the war had ended, Lincoln's opposition to Democratic President James Polk had not. The campaign to choose his successor was underway. Lincoln took to the floor of the House in June and spoke against President Polk's recent veto of a Whig sponsored bill passed by the last Congress, calling for funding of internal improvements across the nation.

***

Mary Lincoln had been enjoying her time back in Lexington, Kentucky. She renewed her ties with her sisters and other relatives, and was able to relax in the **family mansion**, relieved of most of her motherly duties by the household staff. She must have been pleased when, in April, she received a letter from her husband telling her how he missed her and the boys.

When you were here I thought you hindered me some in attending to business; but now, having nothing but business – no variety – it has grown exceedingly tasteless to me...I hate to stay in this old room by myself.[6]

In June, Mary wrote to her husband and told him that she was anxious to return to him in Washington. Time apart had washed away any bad feelings between them. Lincoln replied, "Come as soon as you can. I want to see you and our dear, dear boys very much." By late July the family was together again in their little room at the Sprigg's boarding house.

The couple had exchanged many letters during this period away from each other, but few remain. Robert Lincoln, in the 1920's, burned many that he felt were too personal to allow public scrutiny. In the few letters that did survive, the couple is seen to be lighthearted, joking with each other, sometimes sentimental and almost dreamy in their musings. In one letter Mary teased her husband about how long they had been apart, saying that little Eddie might have forgotten his father. Lincoln took the tease seriously and replied to Mary, who quickly reassured him that both Robert and Eddie still remembered and loved their father.

Some historians suggest that Abraham Lincoln was a tormented man, trapped in a loveless marriage to a shrewish harpy. I believe that the record shows that Mary and Abraham had a loving relationship, perhaps not the burning romantic love typical of youth, but instead a solid, secure love that offered both parties a safe shelter from the storms of life.

***

After only one year in office, Abraham Lincoln was a lame duck legislator. The "rotation" system agreement he had made three years before required that he not stand for re-election. Up to the very end he hoped that the Whigs of the 7th Congressional district would not be able to settle on a candidate to take his place, but they did. Stephen Logan, his former law partner was chosen, in the belief that Lincoln had so badly damaged his standing with the voters of the district due to his vocal opposition to the war, that he could not be re-elected. Logan would give the Whig party a better chance to win the district again. In August, Lincoln received disturbing political news from back home. Stephen Logan had been defeated in the contest for Lincoln's seat. Lincoln attributed the results to the fact that Logan's opponent, a Major Harris, had an appealing record of having served in the army during the war. "That there is any political change against us in the district I cannot believe."[7]

The Taylor campaign asked Congressman Lincoln to travel to the northeast on a speaking tour designed to drum up support for Zachary Taylor for President. Mary was thrilled when her husband asked her and the children to accompany him on the trip. The Lincolns travelled

165

by train, boat and carriage throughout the east for all of September. Their itinerary included speeches in Baltimore, Maryland; Worchester, Boston, Lowell, Taunton, Dorchester, Chelsea, Dedham, Cambridge, and New Bedford, Massachusetts. In his final appearance on the east coast speaking tour, Lincoln shared the stage and speaking honors in Boston with another Whig, Governor William Seward of New York, who was rapidly gaining recognition as a national leader of the Whig party. A local newspaper, the Boston Atlas, covered the event, reporting that Lincoln

...spoke for about an hour, and made a powerful and convincing speech...The audience then gave three hearty cheers for 'Old Zach,' three more for Governor Seward, and three more for Mr. Lincoln, and then adjourned; thus ended one of the best meetings ever held in this good, Whig city.[8]

The Lincoln family boarded a train and headed to Albany, New York, where Abraham met with Millard Fillmore, Zachary Taylor's Vice-Presidential running mate, and with Thurlow Weed, boss of the powerful New York Whig political machine. Lincoln was growing beyond his previous status as a provincial Illinois politician, making important contacts on this trip, ones that would be very valuable to him in the future.

From Albany the family boarded the steamer Globe, and became tourists, stopping at Niagara Falls to marvel at the natural splendor of its roaring waters. They traversed the Great Lakes and disembarked in Chicago, Illinois, where they checked in at the Sherman House hotel. On October 6th, Lincoln addressed a huge crowd gathered in the city's public square, speaking for two hours. The Chicago Journal described the speech as "one of the very best we have ever heard or read since the opening of the campaign."

Similar to today's cable news channels, newspapers of Lincoln's day were generally very partisan. Whereas Whig papers universally praised his efforts, Democratic papers were not so kind. Of a speech he made in Peoria, Illinois, while nearing the end of his month long speaking trip, the Democratic Free Press reported,

Lincoln blew his nose, bobbed his head, threw up his coat tail, and in the course of two hours, was delivered of an immense amount of 'sound and fury.'[9]

On October 10, 1848, the exhausted Lincoln family returned home to Springfield, Illinois. The Springfield Register, a Democratic newspaper, reported on their return.

Hon. Abraham Lincoln...arrived at home at Tuesday last. We are pleased to observe that his arduous duties since the adjournment of Congress, in franking and loading down the mails with Whig electioneering documents, have not impaired his health. He looks remarkably well.[10]

After a brief three weeks at home with his wife and children, Lincoln set out on the campaign trail once again, this time focusing on his home state of Illinois. He was determined to do all he could to see Zachary Taylor elected President, and he hoped that his vigorous support would be seen, appreciated and rewarded by a Taylor administration.

After four weeks speaking all over central Illinois, Lincoln came home to Springfield on November 7[h], and cast his vote for Zachary Taylor for President. By the next day, a bitter President James K. Polk, who had chosen not to run for re-election, acknowledged in his personal diary that his chosen successor, Lewis Cass, had been defeated.

Information received by telegraph...indicates the election of General Taylor. Without political information and without experience in civil life, he is wholly unqualified for the station.[11]

***

In early December, Lincoln travelled back to Washington D. C. to attend his final session of Congress. He was determined to gain some patronage appointments to federal government jobs for his supporters, and perhaps one for himself that would challenge him and expand his influence within the Whig party. That task, along with the everyday work of Congressman would not allow him much time for his family, so Mary and the children remained in Springfield, until his future in Washington became clearer.

Soon after he arrived in Washington, Lincoln received a letter from his father Thomas. They did not normally correspond. He had rarely seen his father since they said their goodbye's back in Decatur, Illinois in the 1830's. Thomas wrote to ask his son for money. Thomas had owed a debt to someone, and that person, not receiving payment, had asked the courts to issue a judgement against Thomas for the $20 debt. Thomas claimed that he had forgotten about the judgement, and now the courts were threatening to sell his lands if he did not pay it immediately. Thomas explained to his son that he did not have the money to cover the judgement. Lincoln's reply to his father, its tone and content, reveal the cold and distant relationship they had.

I cheerfully send you the twenty dollars, which sum you say is necessary to save your land from sale. It is singular that you should have forgotten a judgement against you; and it is more singular that the plaintiff should have let you forget it for so long...Before you pay it...be sure you have not paid.[12]

In the same letter Lincoln had received from his father, written for Thomas Lincoln by Abraham's step-brother, John D. Johnston, his step-brother also asked for money, $80. Lincoln replied to Johnston by telling him that his problem was idleness, and offered him a deal. If Johnston would get work and earn money for the next four months, Lincoln would match the amount he earned and send him that amount. There is no record of whether or not Johnston took Lincoln up on the offer.

In the closing months of his term in Congress Abraham Lincoln consistently voted on the issue of slavery according to the beliefs he had adopted over the past decade. He believed that the federal government had no Constitutional authority to meddle with slavery in the states where it already existed. He also believed that the Constitution did not stipulate that the federal government must allow the expansion of slavery beyond where it already existed. He constantly strove to convince Southerners that their slave owners should accept monetary compensation for their slaves in return for their emancipation, and hoped that these freed slaves might be relocated to their ancestral homes in Africa, or perhaps to a section of the United States specially designated for them. During January of 1849, as Congress dealt with several attempts to ban slavery in Washington D. C. and in the new lands acquired as a result of the war with Mexico, Lincoln held to these beliefs.

With President-elect Taylor's Whig administration readying to take over the government after four years of Democratic rule, job seekers were flooding into the capitol to lobby for federal positions. In February, Lincoln complained to his friend David Davis that he had received over 300 letters inquiring about the job of Commissioner of the Land Office. He was thinking about asking the incoming President for that job for himself, as his term in office was to end in one month. He explained to Davis that he thought he could get the appointment for himself, but as "every man in the state, who wants it himself, would be snarling at me about it, I shrink from it."[13]

William Kolasinski

Chapter Eleven

EARNING A LIVING

Abraham Lincoln's term as a Congressman was over, but he was not yet done in Washington D. C. On March 5th, he attended the inauguration of Zachary Taylor, and the inaugural ball that followed. He spent the evening circulating about the hall saying his goodbyes to fellow Whig Congressmen and Senators, and did not finish until the ball ended at 4am. When he went to the coat check to gather his belongings, he found that his hat had been stolen. Hatless, Lincoln walked back to his room at the Spriggs boarding house.

Lincoln kept busy for the next three weeks by working to secure government positions for Illinois supporters and friends. 3,400 jobs held by Democrats were to be filled by Whigs, and the new President and his cabinet officers were dealing with mountains of letters and swarms of callers, all seeking one of those jobs. It was the first nightmare each newly elected administration needed to face.

Lincoln had failed to get his friend Edward Baker a position in the President's cabinet, so now he lowered his aim. He sent a letter to President Taylor's Secretary of State endorsing Baker for a position as agent to the newly created territory of California, saying that Baker's political skills could help bring California into the Union as a Whig state. He then dispatched a letter to the Secretary of the Treasury requesting that Baker and he, the leading Whigs in Illinois, be consulted when any appointments were awarded to Illinois men.

On March 25th, 1849, Abraham Lincoln departed Washington D.C. and headed back to Springfield, Illinois. None of his lobbying work had yet produced the desired result of a Lincoln sponsored Illinois man getting a federal patronage job.

***

Springfield had changed since Lincoln had left it just two years before. Cow pastures he had once crossed on his way to work were now filled with cottages enclosed by wooden fences. There were large brick houses filled with fine china where the log cabins of early residents once stood. There were not one, but two new hat shops competing for trade, and a new undertaker, who also made cabinets and furniture. Two saddle-makers were now open for business, offering the latest in saddles, harnesses, whips, horse collars, bridles and plows. Fancy saloons offered the hungry patron "oysters, sardines, and other fixins."[1]

Abraham and Mary got busy cleaning their little 1 ½ story cottage. It wore a fresh coat of paint, with white siding, green shutters and white chimneys. As he worked in their little carriage house behind the cottage, applying a fresh coat of axle grease to their buggy wheels and curry-combing their horse, Lincoln may have thought about his barrel-chested, blue-eyed, Democratic opponent in Illinois politics, Stephen Douglas, who now sat in Congress as a U.S. Senator, conferring with his colleagues on matters of state. Some jealousy and regret must have tinged that recollection.

***

The Illinois State Journal carried an advertisement announcing Abraham Lincoln and William Herndon as "attorneys and counselors at law," ready to do business together again. Lincoln was determined to spend his time earning a living in private practice, and providing a good life for his wife and family.

Starting in March and ending in September, then beginning again in February and continuing through June, Lincoln left home to ride the Eighth Judicial Circuit, now covering fourteen counties across central Illinois. Practicing law was his primary focus, but try though he would to focus on building his law practice, politics and Washington D. C. were never completely out of his thoughts. He continued to send letters to officials in the Taylor administration, seeking to obtain jobs for deserving Illinois Whigs. The appointment for the lucrative position ($3,000 annual salary) of Commissioner of the Land Office had not yet been made, and Lincoln was pressing the argument for Cyrus Edwards of Illinois to get the job. He confided to his political associates that if it became clear that Edwards could not get the job, he would ask for it for himself, rather than see it go to the other Whig being considered for it, Justin Butterfield. On May 8, He wrote to a friend about the possibility of Butterfield getting the appointment,

In the great cause of /40 he was not to be seen or heard of; but when the victory came , three or four old drones, including him, got all the valuable offices...Try to defeat B. and in doing so, use Mr. Edwards...or myself, whichever you can to best advantage.[2]

A week later, Lincoln received letters from contacts in Washington D.C. informing him that the rumors were strong in the capitol that Justin Butterfield would soon be named to the post of Commissioner of the General Land Office. They urged Lincoln to act and act quickly to avert defeat. He redoubled his efforts to recruit influential Illinoisans to write letters to the Taylor administration endorsing him for the post.

By June 2, the endorsement campaign seemed to have made an impact, for Lincoln learned that President Taylor had decided to delay filling the Land Office job for three weeks. Lincoln then made a decision to travel to Washington D.C. and lobby for the job in person. Justin Butterfield, in Chicago, made the same decision. By June 10th, both men left by train for Washington D.C.

Exactly what Lincoln and Butterfield did in Washington to further their cause is not known, but on June 21, 1849, President Taylor appointed Justin Butterfield to the position. Upon learning of his failure, Lincoln walked to his rooming house, threw himself down on the bed and remained there for hours.[3]

This was a painful defeat for Lincoln. He had publicly failed in attempts to secure patronage positions for Illinois Whigs in the Taylor administration, and then failed in a very public attempt to gain a position for himself.

Four days later Lincoln departed Washington and returned to Springfield, Illinois.

By the end of July, 1849, Lincoln sent his last letters to the Taylor administration seeking jobs for his fellow Illinois Whigs. He had worked hard for well over a year to further the election of Zachary Taylor to the Presidency, and had little to show for it. Just as he was about to put thoughts of Washington politics behind him, he received a job offer from the Taylor administration. Would he consider being appointed Secretary of the Oregon Territory? As he did with most major political decisions he faced, he sat down to discuss it with his wife. If she found it acceptable, he would consider it further. She responded with a quick and emphatic "No." She did not relish the thought of leaving her friends and relatives, and the comforts of city life in Springfield, to see her husband take up such an obscure position in the barely civilized far west. Lincoln agreed with her that this was an honor he could do without, and so informed the Taylor administration he was not interested. He urged them to consider his friend, the editor of the "Sangamo Journal", Simeon Francis, instead. His focus now needed to be providing a comfortable life for his family.

***

Lincoln and William Herndon began to tend to their growing list of clients in the courts of the Eighth Judicial district. Over the next few years Lincoln fell into the familiar routine of travelling courthouse to courthouse, dealing with many types of legal cases typical of the times: divorces, debt settlements, child custody, bankruptcy, foreclosures, land title disputes.

Sometime in 1850, while he was away on the circuit, his oldest son, Robert Lincoln, ingested some lime, which the family had stored for use in their privy. He became violently ill, and terrified his mother, who, according to neighbors, ran about the house shouting "Bobby will die, Bobby will die, Bobby will die."[4]

Mary Lincoln was quite high strung, and suffered from fears that could occasionally overwhelm her. The fact that she had to face these fears without support from her husband a great deal of the time made her life all the harder. Male neighbors reported that she would come to their homes crying, asking them to stay with her and her boys overnight, because she feared that some strangers she had seen in the neighborhood were planning to break into her house. When thunderstorms struck, she could go into hysterics, begging the neighbors or their children to come to her home and sleep in bed with her and her boys, offering to pay them to do so.

Despite enduring these hardships, Mary soldiered on, keeping house and home clean and presentable while her husband earned them the monies needed to keep up the image of a prospering lawyer's family.

Tragedy and death began to visit the Lincoln's in late 1849. Eddie Lincoln, the three year old, had always been a sickly boy. In 1848 he fell ill twice. The exact nature of these illnesses was not recorded. In December of 1849 he became ill again. He raged with fever, seemed to recover, then fell into lethargy, unable to gather enough strength to get up and play with his brother. Around that same time, Mary received word that her beloved father, Robert Todd, had died of cholera while campaigning for a seat in the Kentucky senate. Then, while Eddie was still in bed sick, she learned that her grandmother

Parker had died from the same cholera outbreak. She was still grieving these deaths when Eddie's fever spiked again. After a 52 day struggle, the little boy died on February 1, 1850. Abraham Lincoln bent over the bed where Eddie was laid out, and hugged the cold, still body of his three year old son for the last time, and then did his best to comfort his distraught wife.

In previous years, the death of one so close to him would have drawn Lincoln into a dark place, but he responded differently to Eddie's death. He submersed himself in his work. Lincoln was learning to accept hardships, not as punishment or as signs of a deity displeased with his actions, but as preordained acts, inevitabilities, that he could not fight, but must learn to endure.

Mary Lincoln, while outwardly professing the same philosophy of predestination as her husband, chose to rail against fate, and even to defy it. While Lincoln's chosen course would bring him some measure of peace through resignation, her course would bring her unending questioning of God and fate, and much emotional distress as she tried to undo what she saw as wrongs befalling her. Within three weeks of losing young Eddie Lincoln, Mary was pregnant again. Even in Mary's day, housewives had several methods to control their reproductive cycle. Mary chose not to. If God or fate took a child from her, then she would smother that grief with the joy of a new life growing inside her.

The four months following Eddie's death found Lincoln handling over 60 cases, some quite involved, some very routine. While the predictable rhythms of life on the circuit soothed Lincoln's injured spirit and allowed him to regain some emotional equilibrium, he was still struggling with his failure to leave any legacy from his term in Congress, and from his life to date. On a carriage ride to Petersburg, Illinois with his partner, William Herndon, he ruminated on what he had accomplished, or failed to accomplish in his life.

How hard, oh, how hard it is to die and leave one's country no better than if one had never lived for it! The world is dead to hope, deaf to its own death struggle, made known by a universal cry, What is to be done? Is anything to be done? Who can do anything? And how is it to be done? Do you ever think of these things? [5]

His time on the circuit, often alone riding between towns, gave him the opportunity to think about how his life had begun, and where the fates had taken him. In a book of exercises in Greek syntax that he owned, he had boxed in a quote that obviously meant something to him.

Deliberate slowly, but execute promptly, the things which have appeared unto thee proper to be done. Love not the immoderate acquisition, but the moderate enjoyment of present good. [6]

He knew that other challenges would come his way, and he believed that he had survived this long for a reason. He would keep searching for that reason and be ready when it showed itself.

***

By early summer, talks about off- year Congressional elections were beginning. In June of 1850, three Illinois newspapers, the Tazewell Mirror, the Western Whig and the Peoria Press, editorialized about Abraham Lincoln as a fitting candidate to run against the incumbent Democrat, Major T. L. Harris, for the 7th district Congressional seat. This surprised Lincoln, as he had so recently been forced by negative public opinion to give up his chance for re-election to that seat in Congress over his stand against the Mexican war. But the war was over and the political landscape was rapidly changing.

New political leaders supporting new issues were appearing in the national newspaper headlines. Democrat Stephen Douglas of Illinois argued for the building of railroads as a means of tying the nation more tightly together despite its growing divisions over slavery. He envisioned a railroad extending from Chicago into the south, all the way to the Gulf of Mexico, and another spanning the continent from the east coast to the territories newly gained from Mexico that bordered on the Pacific shore. William Seward, now the Whig

Governor of New York, Salmon Chase, Senator from Ohio, and the powerful newspaper editor, Horace Greely, were vying for leadership of the growing anti-slavery movement. Jefferson Davis was gaining influence in the Senate and across the South as a champion of state's rights and the South's cherished institution of slavery. Lincoln had been silent for the past two years on these issues as he pursued his livelihood in law.

While in Chicago working on a client's case, Lincoln received news that delayed his considerations about whether or not to run for a second term in Congress. Zachary Taylor had died, after serving only a year and a half as President of the United States. Two weeks later, officials in the city of Chicago asked Lincoln to deliver the eulogy at a mass gathering to honor the late President, in two days' time. After some hesitation, for Lincoln was still bitter over the Taylor administration's treatment of him, he agreed to make the speech. His hastily prepared remarks were well received by an overflow crowd in the city square.

When the Whigs of central Illinois gathered in early August to choose their candidate for the 7th Congressional district, Abraham Lincoln asked them to withdraw his name from consideration. He did not feel the time was right for him, and wanted the Whigs to choose a candidate more likely to garner the support necessary to defeat the incumbent Democrat, Harris. They went on to choose Richard Yates, who defeated Harris in the election.

One of the reasons for Lincoln's decision to withdraw from the race for Congress was the health of his wife, Mary. She was in her last months of pregnancy, preparing for the birth of their third child. On December 21, 1850, she gave birth to **William Wallace Lincoln,**

whom she named after her brother-in-law who had provided much appreciated emotional support to Abraham and Mary during Eddie Lincoln's illness.

Both of Willie's parents were thrilled to hear his cries fill their house. The commotion lifted their spirits and eased their pain over Eddie's death. But that feeling did not last as long as they hoped. On January 10th Lincoln received a letter from Harriet Hanks, daughter of his cousin Dennis, explaining that Thomas Lincoln was very ill, and was not expected to live long. Harriet asked that Lincoln please come as soon as possible. His reply again reveals the emotional distance between father and son.

My business is such that I could hardly leave home now, if it was not as it is now, that my own wife is sick-a-bed. (It is a case of baby-sickness, and I suppose, is not dangerous) I sincerely hope father may recover his health, but at all events, tell him to remember to call upon and confide in our great and good merciful Maker, who will not turn away from him in any extremity. He notes the fall of a sparrow, and numbers the hairs of our heads, and he will not forget the dying man who puts his trust in him. Say to him that if we could meet now, it is doubtful whether it would not be more painful than pleasant, but that if it be his lot to go now, he will soon have a joyous meeting with many loved ones gone before, and where the rest of us, through the help of God, hope ere long to join them.[7]

Thomas Lincoln died on January 17, 1850. Scholars have observed that he had a much closer bond with his step-son, John D. Johnston, than he ever had with his own son, Abraham Lincoln. Thomas never met any of his grandchildren, or his daughter-in-law. His son Abraham never brought them out to Thomas's Coles County farm for a visit, even though he himself stopped in a few times while Thomas Lincoln was alive.

In May, 1851, Abraham came out to the farm near Charleston, Illinois to visit his step-mother and make arrangements with his step-brother, John D. Johnston, for her ongoing support. Four months later, Lincoln agreed to turn over the deed to 80 acres of the 180 acre farm which he had inherited upon his father's death, to his step-brother, with the proviso that **Sara Bush Johnston Lincoln**, his step-mother, would receive his help as needed. Johnston agreed to the deal.[8]

The deal Lincoln believed was in place between John Johnston and him to secure his step-mother's future soon became less settled than he first thought. In November he learned that Johnston was trying to sell his newly acquired 80 acre parcel of the farm and move to Missouri. Angered by his step-brother's decision, he quickly sent him a scolding letter.

When I came into Charleston day before yesterday, I learned that you are anxious to sell the land where you live and move to Missouri. What can you do in Missouri better than here? Your thousand pretenses for not getting along better are all nonsense-they deceive no body but yourself. GO TO WORK is the only cure for your case.[9]

Lincoln and Johnston exchanged more letters on the subject, and finally Lincoln agreed with Johnston's plan,

...if the land can be sold so that I get three hundred dollars to put in interest for mother, I will not object if she does not. But before I will make a deed, the money must be had, or secured, beyond all doubt, at ten percent.[10]

A year later, having sold the portion of Thomas Lincoln's farm that Abraham had deeded to him, John D. Johnston moved to Arkansas. By then, Abraham had placed enough money in the bank on her behalf to ensure that his step-mother Sarah would never be in financial need.

***

In the early 1850's Lincoln became a legal representative for two new businesses that represented the future of transportation in the United States, canal companies and railroads. As farming and manufacturing grew across the country, the demand for the goods they produced grew with them. Canals and railroads were formed to transport goods great distances at a much cheaper price than by previous means. Producers and consumers would now be linked more tightly than ever. With the expansion of these businesses came lawsuits over rights of way, land titles, freight charges, injuries and accidents. Lincoln and Herndon became a leading firm representing these transportation companies in court. This was a lucrative addition to their client list.

Presidential politics distracted Lincoln from legal work in the summer of 1852. Whigs had held the Presidency with Zachary Taylor until his untimely death, then continued their grip on power in Washington with Millard Fillmore, who performed more ably than anyone had expected. Fillmore, who had gained the Presidency not by election but by the death of Zachary Taylor, was not considered a strong candidate for election on his own, so the party prepared to choose a new man to lead them to victory.

The Whig party of Illinois appointed Abraham Lincoln a member of the National Committee that would help make that choice. The party chose General Winfield Scott, a hero of the War of 1812 and the Mexican War, as their candidate. Like Zachary Taylor, Scott was a lifelong military man, who had taken no public position on many of the issues being debated around the country. Whigs, Lincoln included, believed that General Scott could be presented as a man above petty partisan politics, who could unite the country. Lincoln, who had committed so much of his time, energy and reputation to the election of Zachary Taylor with little or no personal advancement to show for his efforts, was not about to put his legal career on hold again. He would only work for Scott's campaign when his schedule of court cases permitted him the time.

The Democrats, after a rancorous convention, chose Franklin Pierce, a Senator from New Hampshire, as their candidate. Stephen Douglas, who had become the leader of movement know as Young America, had been one of the leading candidates for the nomination in a close contest against party veterans who represented a faction he styled as Old Fogyism. Despite the strenuous efforts of Douglas and his supporters, he could not gain the two-thirds majority vote needed to secure the nomination, and eventually helped to steer the convention to choose Pierce as the first "dark horse" to win a Presidential nomination. Pierce was well liked in the Senate, had a military service record, and was a northerner who was sympathetic to Southern positions on state's rights and slavery. Douglas began to campaign vigorously for Pierce in Illinois.

Lincoln made several speeches during the campaign, almost exclusively in Illinois. Whenever Douglas gave an address, Lincoln would make one opposing the Democrat's assertions.

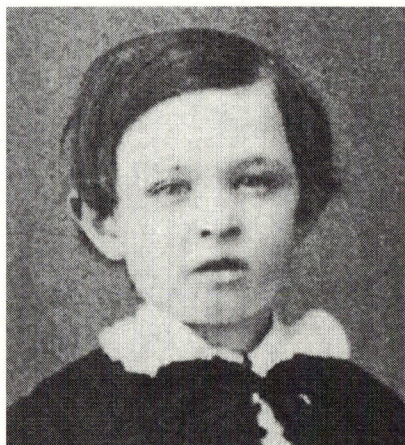

Despite Lincoln's efforts, Winfield Scott lost the state of Illinois to Franklin Pierce, and was soundly beaten in the general election. Lincoln lost little time focusing on growing his client base for the firm of Lincoln and Hendon. He had more reason than ever to do so, for on April 4, 1853, Mary Lincoln gave birth to their fourth child, another son, who they named **Thomas**, after Lincoln's late father.

The delivery was especially difficult for Mary, as Thomas, or Tad (short for his family nickname, Tadpole), had an unusually large head, and Mary was seriously injured during the delivery. The effects of the difficult birth lingered for years, and Mary would not have another child.

***

What is notable about Abraham Lincoln during the years from 1849-1853 is his emotional stability. Despite his being denied another term in the House of representatives, his failure to secure patronage jobs for his supporters from the Taylor administration that he had worked so hard for, the death of his son Eddie and his father, Lincoln did not succumb, as he had in the past, to the darkness of depression. His marriage gave him emotional support that he had not enjoyed before, and his legal and political work occupied his mind so thoroughly that his inner demons were denied a hold on his thoughts. His adoption of a philosophy that viewed personal and professional hardship as inevitable events, not to be fought but to be accepted as learning experiences, also proved crucial to maintaining his emotional equilibrium.

William Kolasinski

Chapter Twelve
OUT OF THE WILDERNESS

T he whole country seemed to be in motion in 1854. In one week that year, twelve thousand emigrants arrived in Chicago, in search of a brighter future. **Springfield** saw its share of "movers," as pioneers were called in those days. A local newspaper reported that in one month 1,473 wagons filled with "movers" departed from capitol square, just below the windows ofLincoln's law office, for lands across the Mississippi River, where

they hoped to establish new homesteads. Hotels in central Illinois were frequently full to capacity with families moving from somewhere to somewhere else. When Abraham Lincoln was in Bloomington, Illinois on business he could not find a vacancy at any hotel, and was forced to search private homes for available lodging.[1]

On January 30, 1854, Stephen A. Douglas, chairman of the Senate Committee on Territories, announced to that body the completion of the Kansas-Nebraska Bill. It would be sent to the House for further debate, and begin a ripple effect of political chaos far greater than the Illinois Senator could have imagined.

Local and national newspapers were filled with articles about Congress and its heated debates over the Kansas-Nebraska bill, and people were beginning to take sides. Those who opposed passage of the bill were referred to as Anti-Nebraska. Those who supported it were "Pop- Sov's" (a shortened version of the Popular Sovereignty provision of the bill championed by Douglas). The bill split the enormous Nebraska Territory into two, Nebraska to the north and Kansas to the south. The citizens of each new territory could vote slavery up or down as they saw fit. This, Senator Douglas explained, was the essence of popular sovereignty. Adoption of this bill would effectively repeal the Missouri Compromise, which for the past 30 years had prohibited slavery from expanding into the unorganized territories of the Great Plains north of the 36-30 parallel (the southern border of the state of Missouri). The Compromise had kept a lid on the debate over of the expansion of slavery, making sure it would not boil over into violence. On May 30, 1854, President Franklin Pierce signed the Kansas-Nebraska bill into law. Now the lid was off the pot.

The more Lincoln studied the Kansas-Nebraska Act that Douglas had ramrodded through Congress, the angrier he grew. He knew that Douglas was determined to organize the west into territories and rapidly bring them into the Union as states, and he knew that the chief reason for Douglas's doing so was to allow for the building of transcontinental railways that would speed the realization of Douglas' dream of a mighty America stretching from ocean to ocean. That was the capstone of his Young America movement within the Democratic Party, and it was his best hope of gaining the 1856 Democratic nomination for President. He hoped that his concept, popular sovereignty, would appeal to Southerners bent on expanding slavery. They could now hope to see it spread throughout the west. He also hoped he could hang on to Northern support by insisting that under Kansas-Nebraska Act Congress would not allow slavery into the territories. It would be up to the people whether slavery was allowed into their territory or not. Lincoln was not amused by Douglas' political maneuvers, but he was not yet sure what he was willing to do to stop them from succeeding.

In July, Cassius Clay, a well- known Kentucky abolitionist, and one of the seemingly endless line of cousins of Mary Lincoln, came to Springfield. He spoke for over two hours about the horrors of slavery. Lincoln lay in the shade of a tree nearby, listening, weighing the man's arguments, while whittling a piece of wood.

By August, Lincoln seemed to have determined his plan of action. He would do everything he could to help elect Anti-Nebraska men to the Illinois legislature. To aid in that effort, he reluctantly allowed himself to be named as a candidate for re-election to the Illinois House of Representatives. This would give him a legitimate reason to campaign around the state and speak against Douglas's Kansas-Nebraska Act. He hoped his presence on the campaign trail would help to draw more Anti-Nebraska voters to the polls.

Lincoln sent a letter to John M. Palmer, a Democratic Congressman, in September, asking him to explain to the people of Illinois his vote in opposition to the Kansas-Nebraska Act:

Is it not just to yourself that you should in a few public speeches, state your reasons (for opposing the Nebraska bill) and thus justify yourself? I wish you would; and yet I say 'don't do it' if you think that it will injure you.[2]

The Kansas-Nebraska Act was causing fissures in the Democratic Party. Lincoln was trying to lead Democrats who stood against slavery expansion, away from their party, and into a sympathetic union with other Anti-Kansas-Nebraska voters.

Lincoln began work to build support among recent immigrants. This was a new strategy for Whigs. Democrats had for many years successfully built a solid core of support amongst the waves of Irish immigrants coming to America. On September 16, Lincoln spoke to a large gathering of German-Americans who were holding an Anti-Nebraska meeting in Bloomington, Illinois. He would continue to build on this relationship with German-Americans for the rest of his political career.

Stephen Douglas was enduring the harshest criticism he had ever experienced as a result of the Kansas-Nebraska Act. Many Southerners, Democrats as well as Whig, were mad at him for not going far enough to ensure the spread of slavery. Northerners from both parties were equally incensed that the Act gave hope to slave owners to expand their culture west.

Douglas decided to travel back home to Illinois to fight for support for his new law. On the train heading west from Washington, he passed by many towns where he saw burning effigies of himself lighting the way. He read stories in local newspapers about how his middle name, Arnold, was derived from the American Revolutionary War traitor's name, Benedict Arnold. In Chicago he was booed off the stage as he tried to explain his Kansas-Nebraska Act. As Senator Douglas left the stage he shouted to the crowd, "It is now Sunday morning – I'll go to church, and you may go to hell." The Chicago Daily Democrat reported of the event,

The spirit of a dictator flashed from out of his eye, curled upon his lip, and mingled its cold irony in every tone of his voice and every gesture of his body.[3]

The state fair began in Springfield, Illinois in early October every year, as a celebration of the completion of another year's harvest. It always drew large crowds to the capitol, but in 1854, the crowds were particularly great. Stephen Douglas and Abraham Lincoln were expected to give speeches of the hot topic of the day – the Kansas-Nebraska Act.

When Senator Douglas came to Springfield, he was greeted by a brass band and a great throng of people who filled the street in front of the Chenery House, where he was to stay. After announcing to the crowd his intention to speak at length the next day at the state capitol, he sought to rally the crowd to his side.

I know the Democrats of Illinois. I know they always do their duty. I know, Democrats, that you will stand by me as you have always done. I am not afraid that you will be led off by renegades from the party...who have formed an unholy alliance to turn the glorious old Democratic Party over to the black Abolitionists. Democrats of Illinois, will you permit it? (Here the crowd roared back, No!) I tell you the time has not yet come when a handful of traitors in our camp can turn the great State of Illinois, with all her glorious history and traditions, into a negro-worshipping, negro-equality community. Illinois has always been, and always will be, true to the Constitution and the Union.[4]

As the crowd roared its approval, he bid them a good night.

On October 3rd, Stephen Douglas spoke to a tightly packed Hall of Representatives at the state capitol building in downtown Springfield. He told the crowd that the heart of the issue about the Kansas-Nebraska Act was "whether the people should rule, whether the voters of a territory should be allowed to control their own affairs?"[5]

A young lady seated next to Lincoln angrily commented that she didn't like the speech Douglas had made. Lincoln replied to her, "Don't bother, young lady. We'll hang the judge's hide on the fence tomorrow."[6]

When Lincoln replied to Douglas the next day, he avoided any personal attack on Douglas. Instead, he targeted the principle of popular sovereignty. He said that it all had to do with whether a Negro was a man or just property.

If he is not a man, in that case he who is a man may, as a matter of self-government, do just what he pleases with him. But if the Negro is a man, is it not to that extent a total destruction of self-government to say that he too shall not govern himself? When the white man governs himself, that is self-government; but when he governs himself and also governs another man that is more than self-government, that is despotism...what I do say is that no man is good enough to govern another man without that other's consent. [7]

William Herndon wrote an account of the speech for the Springfield Journal.

Lincoln quivered with feeling and emotion. The whole house was as still as death. And the house approved the glorious triumph of truth by loud and continued huzzas. Women waved their white handkerchiefs in token of women's heartfelt assent. Douglas felt the sting. He frequently interrupted Mr. Lincoln...It was a proud day for Mr. Lincoln. His friends will never forget it.[8]

Two weeks later, after a similar impassioned address by Lincoln in Peoria, Senator Douglas came to him and said that he (Lincoln) had caused him more trouble over the Kansas-Nebraska Act than all of his enemies in the U. S. Senate. He told Lincoln that if he stopped speaking about the Act during the remaining days of the campaign season, that he, Douglas, would do the same, and return to Washington D.C. Lincoln agreed. Politicians in Illinois and around the country began to take notice of this prairie lawyer who had forced the "Little Giant" to yield on his home ground.

***

In November, Illinois Anti-Nebraska candidates swept to victory in the state elections. Abraham Lincoln was elected to another term in the Illinois legislature and Richard Yates gained a seat in Congress.

Lincoln wasted little time in announcing that he would decline to serve in the state legislature. That had never been his goal. Now that the legislature held a majority of Anti-Nebraska men, he revealed his true goal; a seat in the U. S. Senate, which the legislature had the power to award.

He wrote a letter to a friend, Joseph Gillespie, a lawyer for the Alton Railroad, revealing his thoughts about his future:

I have really got it in my head to try to be a United States Senator, and if I could have your support, my chances would be reasonably good.[9]

He dispatched another letter to Charles Hoyt of Aurora:

Some friends here are really for me, for the U. S. Senate, and I should be very grateful if you could make a mark for me among your members. Please write me giving me the names, post offices and political positions of members round about you.[10]

By early January, Lincoln's efforts to gather support in the legislature seemed to have some effect. He wrote to his friend Elihu Washburne that "I understand myself as having 26 committals; and I do not think any other one man has ten." He then added, prophetically, that "I do not know that it is much advantage to have the largest number of votes at the start."

On February 8th, the Illinois legislature met to elect the next U. S. Senator from Illinois. Lincoln's vote soon reached 47, just 3 short of what he needed to be elected. On the next several ballots, his total began slipping, until it appeared to hit rock bottom with a strong core of only 15 supporters. Lincoln realized that if he hung onto these votes, Governor Joel Matteson, a pro-Douglas, pro- Kansas Nebraska Act Democrat would win. He instructed his supporters to switch their votes to Lyman Trumbull, an Anti-Nebraska Democrat. It was a bitter pill, but he swallowed it. Later he explained to a friend,

I regret my defeat moderately, but I am not nervous about it...The Nebraska men confess that they hate it worse than anything that could have happened.

It is a great consolation to see them worse whipped than I am."

Mary Lincoln took the defeat hard, though she kept the disappointment largely to herself. One immediate casualty of her husband's Senate defeat was her friendship with Julia Jayne Trumbull. As single women and members of the Springfield Coterie of the early 1840's, they had been close friends, and shared many adventures together. Julia had gone on to marry **Lyman Trumbull**, the Democrat who had just bested Lincoln for the Senate seat. Mary suspected Julia, who was as politically astute as she was, of being a very active participant in helping to craft her husband's surprising victory over Lincoln. After 1854, Mary described her former best friend as "ungainly," "cold," "unsympathizing," "unpopular," and a "white sepulcher, " by which phrase she meant to say Julia Trumbull was dead to her.[12]

Such a surprising defeat could have thrown Lincoln into a depression, but it did not. He knew that the release of his votes to Trumbull would be viewed as a selfless act of loyalty, earning him future considerations from Anti-Nebraska forces. He also knew that his speeches against Douglas and the pro- Nebraska forces in the late campaign had gained him wide recognition as a force to be reckoned with in the future. These realizations helped to ease his disappointment.

To demonstrate their lack of bitterness over the defeat for the Senate seat, Abraham and Mary Lincoln hosted a large party at their home on Eighth Street one week later. They invited all the Anti-Nebraska members of the Illinois legislature to attend, regardless of whether they had supported Lincoln or Trumbull. They knew that there would be other opportunities in the future, and they were not about to burn any bridges.

For the balance of the year 1855, Lincoln buried himself in legal work, earning the money he needed to keep his family comfortable. He watched and waited for the political loyalties of Whig, Democrat and Know-Nothing parties (a relatively new organization, strongly opposed to immigrants, whose members, when questioned about being part of the group would respond, I know nothing) to sort themselves out over the newly inflamed issue of slavery extension.

On September 15th, Lincoln responded to a letter from Owen Lovejoy, who had urged Lincoln to join in a fusion party of men who opposed the Kansas-Nebraska Act. Lincoln thought that such a move was premature. He told Lovejoy, "Just now...I fear to do anything, lest I do wrong."

A major legal opportunity came his way in September. McCormick vs. Manny, a legal dispute over patent rights to a reaper design, was being heard in Cincinnati, Ohio. Nationally known east coast attorneys were hired by both sides to argue the case. Lincoln was asked to join the team representing the interests of the Manny Company, as a western attorney who, it was hoped, could provide insight on Midwest courts and customs. The large fee offered, and the chance to partner with two of the brightest legal minds in the country led him to accept the offer. He travelled to Cincinnati, eager to do his best. George Harding and **Edwin Stanton**, the other members of his legal team, after meeting with Lincoln, concluded that he was unkempt, rough mannered, uncouth, and unprepared to face the difficult legal task before the team. They chose to ignore him. Lincoln spent a week in the city, sitting in on the trial, without being asked to contribute anything of importance. When the

193

trial concluded and Lincoln was preparing to depart the city, his hostess at the home where he had been staying told him he was welcome there any time in the future. He replied "I never expect to be in Cincinnati again. I have nothing against the city, but things have so happened here as to make it undesirable for me ever to return."[208] Lincoln would, however, see Mr. Stanton again, under far different circumstances.

Around that same time Lincoln wrote to his old friend, Joshua Speed, whose plantation was just across the Ohio River, south of Cincinnati. Speed, who was now a slave owner, had written him months earlier, asking where he currently stood on the politics of the day. Lincoln replied:

I think I am a Whig, but others say there are no Whigs, and that I am an Abolitionist. I now do no more than oppose the extension of slavery...As a nation, we began by saying 'All men are created equal.' We now practically read it, 'All men are created equal except negroes.' When the Know Nothings get control, it will read 'All men are created equal except negroes, foreigners and Catholics.' The slave breeders and slave traders are a small, odious, and detested class among you, and yet in politics they dictate the course of all of you... [13]

He hoped his position on slavery would not drive a wedge between them. He closed the letter, signing it, "Your friend forever."

***

In 1856, the political loyalties of party supporters across the country were being sorely tested. The Democratic, Whig and Know Nothing (now calling themselves the less insulting name the American Party) parties were all showing signs of being torn apart over the issue of slavery extension. New coalitions were beginning to take shape, ones that included men of like mind on this issue, regardless of their former party affiliation.

In February, a group of Anti- Nebraska newspaper editors gathered in Decatur, Illinois. This meeting marked the beginning of the

Republican Party in the state. Similar meetings were going on across the north. Five months earlier, Lincoln had refused Owen Lovejoy's suggestion to join such a group. This time, while he did not attend the formal meeting, he did attend the dinner that followed, signaling for the first time publicly, that he no longer considered himself a Whig. He would cast his lot with this new Republican Party. At the dinner he was toasted as "our next candidate for the U.S. Senate."

In the early summer the Democratic Party gathered to nominate a candidate for President of the United States. Stephen Douglas was again a leading competitor for it, battling former Congressman and current U. S. Ambassador to England, **James Buchanan.** Douglas entered the convention expecting to win, but he was once again denied the nomination. It went instead to Buchanan. The party felt that Buchanan, a Northern man with strong southern sympathies, could better hold the party together and bring it a victory. The bitter backlash of Southerners against his Kansas-Nebraska Act cost Douglas the prize he had sought for so long.

The newly formed Republican Party gathered in Philadelphia in June, to pick their first Presidential candidate. Its choice of John C. Fremont was not without opposition (Lincoln actually favored Supreme Court Justice John McLean), but was generally viewed as a strong one. Fremont was a national hero, having led expeditions to map and explore the vast lands of the Louisiana Purchase. The surprise came when Abraham Lincoln of Illinois received 110 votes for

Vice-President. He went on to lose to William Dayton, but he was clearly thought of by the leaders of his new party as a man with the potential to be a candidate for national office.

When Lincoln heard the news about his getting 110 votes for Vice-President at the national convention, he made a joke of it, saying that there was a great man in Massachusetts named Lincoln, and he must be the one for whom the votes were cast.[14]

Unlike 1852, when he only made a few speeches in support of the Whig candidate, Winfield Scott, Lincoln campaigned hard all across Illinois for the ticket of Fremont and Dayton, even venturing into Iowa to address crowds there. By Election Day he had given over 40 speeches in support of Republican candidates for office. Fremont lost the election to Buchanan, but put up impressive numbers on behalf of his new party in its first national contest. Republicans in Illinois were jubilant over the victory of their very first candidate for Governor, William Bissell. The Whig party was no more, and it looked like the Republican Party might just succeed in becoming the new national party to oppose the Democrats.

Abraham and Mary Lincoln were in an optimistic mood with the beginning of 1857. They held a large party in February, attended by over 300 people. They then attended a ball, hosted by the new Republican Governor of the state. Mary wrote to her sister, Emilie:

Within the last three weeks there has been a party almost every night and some two or three grand fetes are coming off this week.[15]

Only four months into his term as President, James Buchanan's administration was presented with a decision by the Supreme Court that took the nation by surprise. Dred Scott, a slave who had been taken by his master to live with him in a free state, had sued his master, claiming that by residing in a free state, he was now a free man. Chief Justice Roger Taney, speaking for a majority on the court, declared that Dred Scott was not a man, but rather property, and that his master had the right to bring his property back with him to the slave state from which they had come. President Buchanan himself was not surprised. He had secretly been lobbying the Court, even before his election, to find just as they did. Stephen Douglas chose to support the decision. Republicans were incensed by it.

In June Lincoln spoke to a crowd in the House chamber of the Illinois legislature, arguing that Senator Douglas, President Buchanan, and the Supreme Court were mistaken about the Dred Scott decision. He urged that the court's decision not be considered a precedent.

In September, the Democratic Party suffered a severe test, when the territory of Kansas produced a new constitution that challenged one already existent, written in 1855. That original constitution prohibited slavery in Kansas. A new convention was convened in 1857, in Lecompton, Kansas. It was composed of pro-slavery supporters and it produced a constitution that allowed slavery in the territory. Backers of each constitution insisted that theirs was the "real" and legitimate constitution of the state. President Buchanan strongly supported the new Lecompton constitution, while Stephen Douglas refused to support it, insisting that here had been massive irregularities in the process of creating it. He wanted the people of the territory to vote on what kind of constitution they wanted, per his Popular Sovereignty approach. Buchanan and those who sided with him, mainly southern Democrats, vowed to destroy Douglas for his opposition to their party leader, the President.

Lincoln wrote to Senator Lyman Trumbull in November:

What do you think of the rumpus among the democracy over the Kansas constitution? I think the Republicans should stand clear of it. In their view both the President and Douglas are wrong; and they should not espouse the cause of either, because they may consider the other a little farther wrong of the two.[16]

Lincoln and the Republican Party sensed a real opportunity coming. Douglas would soon have to stand for re-election, and there was every reason to suspect that Douglas' own President would do his best to see the Senator defeated. Lincoln's fear was that some Republicans, in their eagerness to see Buchanan's Kansas policies thwarted, would support Douglas over their own Senate candidate, who, Lincoln sorely hoped, would be himself.

In December he saw his fears becoming reality. Horace Greeley, the powerful editor of the "New York Tribune", a Republican, had been writing editorials in praise of Stephen Douglas' courageous battle against the Buchanan administration. Lincoln wrote to a friend, *"What does the "New York Tribune" mean by its constant eulogizing and admiring and magnifying Douglas?"*[7]

He believed that the editorials could result in thousands of defections by Republican voters to Stephen Douglas' side in the upcoming Senate election.

In April, **Hannah Armstrong**, the wife of Lincoln's old friend, Jack Armstrong, leader of the Clary's Grove boys in New Salem, contacted him to ask for help. Her son, **Duff**, had been involved in a fight, and the man he had been battling had died from a knife wound, said to have been inflicted by Duff. Hanna was desperate. She had little money with which to pay him, but she hoped he would come to defend her son. Lincoln was very fond of the Armstrong family. When he was struggling to make ends meet in New Salem, Hannah would have him over to their cabin, where she would feed him and repair his tattered clothing. He had bounced little Duff on his knee when he was a baby. Upon reading the letter he immediately set out for Beardstown, Illinois, the site of the trial. The case, known to Lincoln buffs as the Almanac Trial, began and ended on May 7, 1858. The prosecution's evidence rested squarely on the testimony of an eye witness, who claimed that he had seen Duff Armstrong argue with and then stab the victim. Even though it was eleven o'clock at night, the witness claimed there was sufficient moonlight for him to observe the incident. Lincoln destroyed the prosecution's case by producing a Farmer's Almanac which indicated that on the night in question the moon had been waning, not waxing, and that there could not have been sufficient moonlight for the witness to have seen what he claimed. The murder charge was dismissed and Duff Armstrong walked out of the courtroom a free man. Lincoln refused to accept any form of payment from Hannah. What she and her late husband had done for him in New Salem had been payment enough.

***

The dispute between Democratic President James Buchanan and Democratic Senator Stephen Douglas over the Lecompton Constitution continued to muddy the political waters in Illinois as the campaign for Douglas' re-election to the U. S. Senate approached.

Some Republicans were hoping to lure Buchanan Democrats over to their side to vote against Douglas. Lincoln wrote to a friend:

I know of no effort to unite the Reps & Buc. Men, and believe there is none. Of course, the Republicans do not try to keep the common enemy from dividing; but so far as I know, or believe, they will not unite with either branch of the division.[18]

Mid- June found the Republicans of Illinois preparing to convene in

Springfield to name a candidate to oppose Stephen Douglas in his bid for re-election to the U. S. Senate. Lincoln was the heavy favorite to receive their endorsement. The night before the convention opened, Lincoln met with several party leaders at the state library, and read them the speech he planned to give the next day if he was nominated. When he reached the paragraph in the address that contained the phrase "...a house divided against itself cannot stand," many of them interrupted him, arguing that it was far too radical a statement. They urged him to delete that portion. Only his law partner William Herndon supported Lincoln. Lincoln decided to keep the paragraph in his speech.

On June 16th, the Republican convention convened in the state House of Representatives and quickly declared "that Abraham Lincoln is the first and only choice of the Republicans of Illinois for the U. S. Senate." That night Lincoln addressed the group and delivered his "House Divided" speech. Lincoln had now emerged from the political wilderness, and was ready to match wits with the best known Democrat in the country.

Mary Lincoln was confident that when the voters of Illinois had the chance to see and hear her husband, he would prevail. Referring to Douglas and his nickname, the "Little Giant," she said to a friend that he was "a very little, little giant by the side of my tall Kentuckian and intellectually my husband towers above Douglas just as he does physically."[19]

Both candidates began a grueling campaign that saw them travel thousands of miles, and give countless speeches to gatherings large and small, all across the Midwest. **Lincoln** started the contest by following **Douglas** on the trail, and giving speeches after Douglas had finished. Eventually the two candidates worked out an agreement in which both agreed to share the same stage, speaking in seven congressional districts around the state, alternating who would address the crowds first. This was believed to be an advantage for Lincoln, who had been having trouble drawing crowds as large as those who came to hear Douglas. The debates garnered headlines all across the nation as the two men laid out their very different visions of how the country should handle the issue of slavery. Douglas argued for the concept of popular sovereignty, refusing to characterize slavery as a good or an evil. He wanted the people of each new territory to decide the issue for themselves. Lincoln argued that slavery was a moral evil, but that its existence in the states that currently allowed it was protected by the constitution. He simply wanted to stop its expansion, believing that the Founding Fathers had always intended for it to eventually die out.

When the contest was over, Democrats had secured enough seats in the Illinois legislature to award Douglas another term in the Senate, even though Lincoln had narrowly won the popular vote. It was a defeat for Lincoln, and he felt the sting of it, saying to friends soon after, "It hurt too bad to laugh, and I am too big to cry."[20]

Sometime after the election, a young girl from Winchester, Illinois named Rosa Haggard asked him to sign her autograph book. Expecting to see a simple signature, Rosa was surprised to read what Lincoln wrote in her autograph book:

To Rosa –

You are young and I am older;

You are hopeful, I am not –

Enjoy life, ere it grows colder –

Pluck the roses, ere they rot.[21]

As he began to reflect on the past contest he could not have been ignorant of the fact that it had made him a nationally known figure, and one of the recognized leaders of the national Republican Party. He said of the loss, somewhat disingenuously, "Though I now sink out of view and shall be forgotten, I believe I have made some marks which will tell for the cause of civil liberty long after I am gone."[22]

Lincoln did go back to practicing law after his second defeat for the Senate, but neither he nor his wife had any intention of him sinking out of sight. During the late Senate campaign, Lincoln had become trapped by a severe thunderstorm in Petersburg, Illinois. He took shelter in a railroad box car with Henry Villard, a correspondent from the New York Staats-Zeitung, a German-American newspaper. The two men shared reminiscences of their youth, and Lincoln explained how, when he was a country clerk in New Salem, all he wished for was to be elected a member of the Illinois legislature. "Since then, of course" he said, "I have grown some." Of his campaign for the Senate he said to Villard, "I am saying to myself every day: 'Is it too big for you? You will never get it.' Mary insists, however, that I am going to be Senator and President of the United States, too". He hugged his knees tight to himself, gave out a loud laugh and told Villard, "Just think of such a sucker as me being President!"[23]

Despite his humility, people were thinking of him as a possible Presidential candidate. He began receiving invitations to speak all over the country. He turned down offers to speak in Massachusetts, Minnesota, and Wisconsin, explaining that his legal work was taking up all his time.

In April of 1859, a Rhode Island newspaper editor sent him a letter asking permission to propose him as a Republican candidate for President in 1860. He replied:

I must, in candor, say I do not think myself fit for the Presidency. I certainly am flattered...but I really think it best for our cause that no concerted effort such as you suggest, should be made.[24]

By July, he had changed his position, if ever so slightly. In reply to a very flattering letter from Samuel Galloway, an influential Ohio lawyer, he wrote, "I must say I do not think myself fit for the Presidency." He issued no request for Galloway to discontinue efforts on his behalf.

In September he reversed his position on speaking engagements outside Illinois, and travelled to Ohio to give speeches in Columbus, Dayton and Cincinnati. In Cincinnati he and Mary stayed with her cousin (yes, yet another one), Mrs. William Dickinson. Mrs. Dickinson was the same woman he stayed with during his embarrassing experience as a lawyer in the McCormick reaper case, during which his own legal team had completely ignored him. He had left town telling Mrs. Dickinson he would probably never return. Now he had come back, as a possible candidate for President of the United States.

On his way home he stopped in Indianapolis to give a speech. Two weeks later he travelled to Wisconsin, speaking in Milwaukee, Beloit and Janesville. Any candidate for the presidential nomination of his party would have to show strength in his home region, and Lincoln certainly seemed to be shoring up his following in the Midwest.

Contrary to popular belief, Lincoln was not a reluctant candidate for President in 1860, or one who did little to gain the nomination, preferring to sit back and let events take their course. He had a plan to stay "under the radar," and in doing so, offend none of the front runners in his party, like William Seward, Salmon Chase, and Simon Cameron. He accomplished this masterfully.

Republicans all around the nation rejoiced on October 14[th,] when the results of state elections in Pennsylvania, Ohio, Indiana and Minnesota were confirmed. Their slates of candidates had won convincing victories. The party was showing that it had broad appeal, and was positioned well to take on the Democrats in the 1860 Presidential election.

In December, 1859, Lincoln had copies of his debates with Douglas bound as a book, and sent to supporters in Ohio, to use as they saw fit. He also composed a brief auto-biography for Jesse Fell, who requested it as something he could send to the many people who were enquiring of him who this man Abraham Lincoln was, that they had been hearing about. He said of it:

Herewith is a little sketch, as you requested. There is not much of it, for the reason, I suppose, that there is not much of me.[25]

***

As Lincoln's non-campaign moved ahead he continued to receive invitations to speak. He had already toured the Midwest and shored up his support there. Now he decided it was time to build his reputation in the east, home to his chief rival for the nomination, William Seward. He accepted an invitation to speak in several east coast cities and to give a major address at the Cooper Union in New

York. The trip would also allow him to visit his son Robert, who was enrolled at Exeter Academy in New Hampshire.

Many of the country's intellectual elite were in the audience on February 27th when Lincoln stepped onto **the stage at Cooper Union** to deliver his address. David Dudley Field, a nationally known lawyer and civil reformer, escorted him to the podium, and William Cullen Bryant, poet and editor, introduced him to the audience. He stood before the well- dressed crowd for a brief moment, as they got their first glimpse of him; tall and thin, with deep set, dark eyes and an unruly mane of coarse black hair, wearing a shiny new black, broadcloth suit still wrinkled from being so long folded in his valise. He began slowly with the words "Mr. Cheerman," spoken with a Kentucky twang strange to their ears.

Two hours later he finished with the words "Let us have faith that right makes might' and in that faith let us to the end dare to do our duty as we understand it." Hats flew into the air, applause and cheers rang through the hall. He had won them over with his words, his passion and his reasoning, despite his strange accent and rumpled suit.

The rest of the east coast trip went as well as the speech in New York.

He was building a following in an area of the country where months before, he had been an unknown. He never referred to party rivals in his speeches, never spoke ill of any man, just laid out his positions in such a way that audiences felt compelled to agree with him.

Lincoln returned to Springfield in mid-March, and shifted into a new phase of his campaign for the nomination. He stopped denying his interest in, or his fitness for the Presidency. He wrote to his friend Samuel Galloway in Ohio:

My name is new in the field; and I suppose I am not the first choice of a very great many. Our policy then, is to give no offence to others - leave them in a mood to come to us, if they shall be compelled to give up their first love.[26]

On April 23, 1860, the Democrats opened their national convention in Charleston, South Carolina. Senator Stephen Douglas of Illinois was expected to be the nominee. The convention had changed its voting rules, and now required the winning candidate to gather 2/3 of the total delegate vote. Southerners, angered that Douglas and his supporters had forced though a platform without a provision guaranteeing slavery expansion into new territories, refused to vote for him. Without southern support Douglas could achieve no more than a solid majority of delegate votes, short of the new 2/3 vote required. After days of deadlock, the convention adjourned, to reconvene eight weeks later in Baltimore, Maryland.

The Democratic Party was showing signs of breaking apart. Further confusing the electoral scene, a new political group appeared, calling itself the Constitutional Union Party. Formed out of disgruntled former Whigs and Know-Nothings, they nominated John Bell of Tennessee as their candidate for President on the platform of "Compromise and Union." Republican prospects for winning the Presidency seemed brighter than they could have ever imagined.

Rail Splitter.

"The People of the United States are the Rightful Masters of both Congress and Courts."—Abraham Lincoln.

CHICAGO, ILL., SATURDAY, OCTOBER 27, 1860. NO. 18.

The Illinois state Republican convention opened in Decatur, Illinois on May 9th. John Hanks, who had travelled with Lincoln down the Mississippi River to New Orleans on a flatboat in 1831, came marching down the main aisle of the convention hall carrying two wooden fence rails with Lincoln for President placards nailed to them, loudly proclaiming that Lincoln had split them himself many years before. Lincoln spoke briefly, acknowledging that they were authentic. The crowd roared its approval, and the nickname **"The Rail-Splitter"** entered the political lexicon. The next day the convention unanimously instructed their delegates to the national convention to vote for Abraham Lincoln for the Republican Presidential nomination.

Lincoln's friends, without any assistance from him, had managed to convince the Republican national committee to hold their nominating convention in Chicago, Illinois. Supporters of the front-runner, Senator William Seward of New York, were confident that the location of the meeting would have little effect on their candidate's powerful hold on a majority of the delegates.

Lincoln, who chose not to attend the convention, instructed his managers to make no binding deals on his behalf. He wanted his candidacy to gain strength as the front runners lost momentum after the first ballot. David Davis ignored Lincoln's wishes, saying he was not on the scene, and could not judge the situation properly. He began to talk with some of the lesser candidates whose names had been put in nomination, suggesting that if, at the right time they released their supporters to vote for their second choice, Lincoln, that a cabinet post or ambassadorship might be in their future. Davis and his friends also made a deal with a local man to manufacture counterfeit admission tickets, and used them to flood the convention floor with Lincoln supporters before Seward's people arrived to take their seats. When the Seward supporters did arrive, marching bands blaring and New Yorkers singing, they found their seats already filled, and were denied entrance to the convention floor. When the balloting began, Seward took the lead, as expected. But he did not gain a majority, so a second ballot started. Lincoln men, who filled most of the seats in the hall, began howling, stomping and yelling for Lincoln, making the convention hall sound to some like the nearby stockyards, where thousands of hogs screamed as they were being led to the slaughter. Delegates took note of the surprising support that the crowd showed for Lincoln, and they began to leave their first choice, Seward, for the Rail-Splitter. By the third ballot it was over. Seward men were in shock. Lincoln had won the nomination.

Abraham Lincoln was in Springfield, playing a game of handball, when a messenger bought him the news. He immediately headed for home to tell Mary, followed by a growing crowd of cheering neighbors and friends. Once home, he shared the news with his wife and children, and then opened the door to as many celebrants as the house would hold.

The Democrats opened their second convention in Baltimore, Maryland on June 18th. John Bell supporters were already campaigning, telling voters that Bell would do whatever was needed to uphold the Constitution and keep the Union together. Abraham Lincoln's surrogates were also spreading out across the north, arguing that Lincoln would not touch slavery where it already existed, but would not allow its extension into any new territories. Southern Democrats pressured Douglas to include a plank in the party platform that called for expansion of slavery. He refused. Southerners, angered at Douglas' intransigence on this all important issue, walked out of the convention, spreading the word that they would reform somewhere else in the city to nominate their own candidate. Douglas forces regrouped after their departure and easily nominated Stephen

Douglas for President with the votes of more than 2/3 of the delegates remaining in the hall. The Southern wing of the Democratic Party met and nominated John C. Breckenridge, President Buchanan's current Vice-President, for the Presidency, on a platform that called for protection of state's rights and unfettered expansion of slavery. The lines were drawn. The campaign of 1860 would offer the country four distinctly different paths into the future.

The next several months saw, **Bell, Lincoln** and **Breckenridge** running campaigns typical of the time. They stayed at home, giving interviews, issuing general statements, and rarely speaking in public. Their campaigns relied on surrogates to go into the field and give speeches explaining their candidate's positions on the issues of the day. Stephen **Douglas** broke with

that tradition, and travelled extensively to address the citizenry in person. With the splitting of his party, he felt that this was his only chance at gaining a victory.

All through the summer and fall, Lincoln remained in Springfield. His law partner, William Herndon wrote to Lyman Trumbull:

Lincoln is doing well. Has thousands of letters daily, many visitors every hour from all sections. He is bored, bored badly.[27]

By August Lincoln was beginning to be cautiously confident. He wrote to his old friend Simeon Francis, former editor of the "Sangamo Journal", who was now living in Oregon,

I hesitate to say it, but it really appears now, as if the success of the Republican ticket is inevitable.[28]

Despite rumors swirling about the nation that summer about secession of the southern states if he were to be elected, Lincoln still believed that it was not inevitable. He wrote to a supporter "...that in no probable event will there be any very formidable effort to break up the Union."

In October, results of the election for state office in Ohio, Pennsylvania and Indiana showed Republicans garnering more votes than they had in 1856. Many won offices away from the Democrats. In Springfield, Lincoln wrote to William Seward:

It now really looks as if the government is about to fall into our hands. Pennsylvania, Ohio and Indiana have surpassed all expectation.[29]

While sifting through the great piles of letters sent to him, Lincoln opened and read a letter from Grace Bedell, a young girl living in Westfield, New York. She asked him about his family, and suggested that he might consider growing a beard, as it would give him a more serious, statesmanlike appearance. He replied to her,

My dear little Miss,

I regret the necessity of saying I have no daughter. I have three sons....They, with their mother, constitute my whole family. As to the whiskers, having never worn any, do you not think people would call it a piece of silly affection if I were to begin it now?[30]

Despite his protestations to Grace, he soon **began to cultivate a beard.**

The rumors of secession that had begun months before were not dissipating, but growing more frequent and worrisome. In late October, Lincoln received reports that upon his election, army officers at Fort Kearny, Nebraska, were going to abandon their posts and travel south, taking what weapons they could with them. Lincoln contacted a friend in the military, Major David Hunter, and asked him to look into the rumor and determine its truth. Secession was now more than just a rumor.

Abraham Lincoln spent the daylight hours of Election Day, November 6th, in his second floor office in the state capitol building, greeting well-wishers and working on correspondence. At 3pm he left to walk over to the courthouse to cast his vote, and then headed to the city telegraph office to await the voting returns. After nine o'clock the results became clear. He had carried Pennsylvania and New York. He had been elected President of the United States. But the results told a disturbing tale of a nation divided. Fifteen states had given him no electoral votes. Ten states in the South had given him not a single vote. His total of the popular vote was 39%. A million more people out of the 4,700,000, who voted, chose someone else.

The huge crowd outside the telegraph office was heard loudly singing a campaign tune sung to the melody of "The Old Gray Mare." It began,

Old Abe Lincoln came out of the wilderness,

Out of the wilderness,

Out of the wilderness,

Old Abe Lincoln came out of the wilderness,

Down in Illinois.

A surprisingly somber President-elect headed home after midnight to tell his wife, "Mary, we are elected."

William Kolasinski

Chapter Thirteen
INTO THE FIERY FURNACE

Even in our sleep, pain that cannot forget falls drop by drop upon the heart, and in our own despair, against our will, comes wisdom to us by the awful grace of God.

Aeschylus

The last years of Abraham Lincoln's life, those of his Presidency, contained so much of historical significance that I was forced to make a decision as to what of it I would include in this chapter. Many great historians have covered the legislative and military battles that transformed our country during those years. I will not try to repeat their work. This chapter will, instead, focus on Lincoln and his family, and the series of deaths, accidents, illnesses and tragedies that afflicted them and forced Lincoln as President to see the Civil War in a different light than when it first began.

***

As Mary Lincoln began packing the family's belongings in preparation for their move to Washington D. C., events were occurring that gave the nation reason to fear for its future. On December 20, 1860, just six weeks after Abraham Lincoln was elected, South Carolina seceded from the Union. President James Buchanan, marking time in the White House until Lincoln's Inauguration on March 4th, did nothing to stop it. He was a strict constructionist in his interpretation of the Constitution and the powers it bestowed on the Chief Executive, and while he believed secession to be wrong, he did not believe that the Constitution gave him any power to stop it.

Lincoln could do nothing to address the secession crisis until he was sworn in, and decided that he would say little until then, believing that any statement he might make could be misconstrued, inflaming the situation even more. He urged Southerners to read his many past speeches on slavery, and in doing so, learn that they need not fear loss of their slave property under a Republican administration.

His sleep became troubled. Years later he told his friend Noah Brooks about a strange thing that had happened on the day after his election. Exhausted, he had thrown himself down onto a lounge chair in his statehouse office:

Opposite where I lay was a bureau with a swinging glass upon it, and looking into that glass I saw myself reflected nearly at full length; but my face, I noticed, had two separate and distinct images, the tip of the nose of one being about three inches from the tip of the other. I was a little bothered, perhaps startled, and got up and looked in the glass, but the illusion vanished. On lying down again, I saw it a second time, plainer, if possible, than before; and then I noticed that one of the faces was a little paler – say five shades, than the other. I got up, and the thing melted away, and I went off, and in the excitement of the hour forgot all about it – nearly but not quite, for the thing would once in a while come up, and give me a little pang, as if something uncomfortable had happened. When I went home again that night I told my wife about it, and a few days afterward I made the experiment again, when sure enough, the thing came back again but I never succeeded in bringing the ghost back after that, though I once tried very industriously to show it to my wife, who was somewhat worried about it. She thought it was a 'sign' that I was to be elected to a second term of office, and that the paleness of one of the faces was an omen that I should not see life through the last term.[1]

A few weeks after the election, hate mail began to arrive at the cottage on Eighth and Jackson Street in Springfield. Mary received a large package sent to her by an unknown person in South Carolina. When she opened it, she saw that it was a painting of her husband with hands and feet bound, hanging from a rope around his neck, covered with tar and feathers. When another letter was opened, it was found to contain a sketch of the Devil stabbing Lincoln with a three-pronged fork and pitching him into the fires of Hell. The graphic hate mail continued to arrive, and along with it came upsetting news that more southern states were planning to secede, form their own country, and elect their own President. Mary knew that her husband was going to Washington D. C. to face the greatest crisis any President had dealt with since George Washington and the Revolution. This would not be the joyous time she had dreamed of as a little girl, with her husband being President, and her enjoying the adulation of the public.

On February 11th, 1861, President-elect Lincoln left his home on Eighth Street in Springfield and rode by carriage to the Great Western train station a few blocks away. Abraham and Mary had quarreled some the day before, with Lincoln trying to convince her to travel separately with the children and join him in Washington after he had gone there first. He was worried by reports he had received about threats of assassination attempts and violence in various cities he was to stop at along the way. Mary insisted that she would remain by his side, come what may. In the end they compromised. Lincoln and his oldest son Robert would depart for Washington first. Mary and the younger children would join him in Indianapolis a few days later.

It was a cold, rainy day, and his sadness at leaving Springfield and all his friends there added to the gloom. The New York Herald reporter Henry Villard, covering the President-elect for his newspaper, reported on the scene as Lincoln arrived sometime after 7am at the small, red brick depot. "His face was pale, and quivered with emotions so deep as to render him almost unable to utter a single word." [2] For forty minutes Lincoln greeted and spoke with some of the one thousand neighbors that had gathered to see him off. Then he left the station building and boarded the train that would take him to Washington D. C., and a capitol reeling with political confusion. From the back of the last car of the train he looked out at his neighbors for the last time, spoke a few lines filled with sadness at the parting and bid them all an "affectionate farewell."

The trip proceeded smoothly. The family was reunited in Indianapolis and they settled in for a two week tour throughout the Midwest and north, with Lincoln speaking at several cities. As the Presidential tour neared Baltimore, Maryland, Lincoln received word from Allan Pinkerton, a detective who Lincoln knew from their days together working for the Illinois Central Railroad, about a plot to assassinate him when he stopped in Baltimore, Maryland to transfer trains for the last part of the journey to Washington. Lincoln trusted Pinkerton, but was hesitant to alter the plans that had been widely published, based on just one set of evidence. As he conferred with his advisors and family and considered what he should do he received another communication, this one from the General of the Army, Winfield Scott. Scott reported that his spies had also uncovered details of a Baltimore plot, well developed and ready to be launched in downtown Baltimore. The weight of the two sets of information, both in agreement on many details, convinced him of the wisdom of altering the travel plan. The truth of these rumored plots was verified later. Had he stuck to his schedule, Lincoln might well have been killed in Baltimore, Maryland. Lincoln had faced death and managed to escape it. He and Mary now knew the awful reality of the dangers he would face over the next five years.

***

The Southern states seceded one by one, until eleven states had declared themselves free of the Union. On February 8, 1861 they joined to form a new nation, calling themselves the Confederate States of America, and elected Jefferson Davis, a U.S. Senator from Mississippi, as their President. On March 4, Abraham Lincoln was sworn in as President of the United States, concluding his **inaugural address** with words directed at the people of the South:

"I am loth to close. We are not enemies, but friends. We must not be enemies. Though passion may have strained, it must not break our bonds of affection. The mystic chords of memory, stretching from every battlefield, and patriot grave, to every living heart and hearthstone, all over this broad land, will yet swell the chorus of the Union, when again touched, as surely they will be, by the better angels of our nature.[3]

Despite Lincoln's plea, the war began soon after, when Confederate forces bombarded Union held Fort Sumter in the harbor of Charleston, South Carolina, on April 12, 1861. The fort was forced to surrender and the Confederacy had its first victory in what both sides believed would be a short war.

Washington D.C. was rapidly becoming an armed camp. On April 15th, President Lincoln issued a call for 75,000 volunteers to report for duty in the Union army. Recruits began filing into the city, and every open space in the District of Columbia was filling with tents, horses and military gear. Drums could be heard beating roll calls each morning, and officers could be seen drilling their men on the White House lawn, working to turn them from farm hands and factory workers into professional soldiers.

The **influx of soldiers**, horses, pigs and other livestock into the capital, made what had been a very unsanitary city, even less healthy. Piles of horse and pig manure dotted the streets and open fields of the city, and mixed with human sewage to create a perfect breeding ground for flies, mosquitoes, rats and disease. The Lincoln's were living in one of the unhealthiest cities in the nation.

Lincoln could see and smell the foulness of **the Washington sanitary canal,** a river of sewage, from his open office windows. Soon after moving into the White House Willie and Tad came down with a severe case of the measles. In early April, with the boys still recovering from that sickness, the entire family fell ill. They had just enjoyed a dinner of fresh Potomac River Shade, a popular Washington D. C. dish, when all of them became nauseous and weak. The fish may have been spoiled, or prepared with contaminated ingredients, or the family may have drunk polluted water from the Potomac River. They were all fully recovered within a week.

The horrors of war had not yet struck home for the Lincolns, but they soon would. **Ellsworth** was a handsome, black haired, hazel eyed, young Illinois man, who had clerked with Lincoln and Herndon at their law office in Springfield. In his off-time from legal work before the war, Ellsworth had formed a group of firemen into a paramilitary unit called the Fire Zouaves (named after their colorful French styled military outfits). They developed a very gymnastic set of drill routines that they performed for audiences around the Midwest. The handsome Ellsworth became something of a

matinee idol, and developed a large following, especially among the young ladies of the country. When the war started he and his troop enlisted and became part of the growing Union army camped in Washington D.C. The Lincoln family was very fond of him. Tad and Willie Lincoln wore little Zouave outfits around the White House, in honor of their hero, Colonel Ellsworth.

On May 24, 1861, one day after Virginia officially seceded from the Union; Colonel Ellsworth led his troops across the Potomac River into Alexandria, Virginia. His objective was to capture the town and cut its telegraph lines. Once across the river, Ellsworth led his men to Marshall's Hotel, where a large Confederate flag that many citizens of Washington, including President Lincoln, could see, was flying from a flagpole on the roof. Ellsworth dashed up the hotel stairs alone and tore the flag from its pole. He tucked it under his arm and was coming back down the stairs when the hotel owner, James T. Jackson, suddenly appeared and fired both barrels of his shotgun into Ellsworth's chest. His Zouave soldiers immediately returned fire, hitting Jackson in the face, and then bayoneted him to death. **Ellsworth died** before they could remove him from the hotel.

Word of the popular Ellsworth's death spread quickly in Washington. President Lincoln was in the White House library on the second floor when he received the news. Just as he did, Senator Henry Wilson and a reporter from the New York Herald entered the room. Lincoln had his back to them, and was staring out at the Potomac River and Alexandria. As he heard them coming toward him he spun around, took a step toward them and then thrust his arm, stopping them. "Excuse me," he said, "but I cannot speak," and then began to cry. After a short time he regained his composure. "I will make no apology, gentlemen, for my weakness, but I knew poor Ellsworth well, and held him in high regard."[4]

That afternoon the President and Mrs. Lincoln went to the Navy Yard to view the body and offer their respects. Lincoln returned alone later that night to sit with the body of his young friend. The next day, he penned a note to Colonel Ellsworth's parents, not knowing it would be the first of many such condolences he would have to send:

My dear Sir and Madam,

In the untimely loss of your noble son, our affliction here is scarcely less than your own. So much of promised usefulness to one's country, and of bright hopes for one's self and friends, have rarely been so suddenly dashed, as in his fall...May God give you that consolation which is beyond all earthly power. Sincerely, your friend in a common affliction, A. Lincoln[5]

***

Less than two weeks after Ellsworth's death, Lincoln lost his great rival, Stephen A. Douglas. After losing the Presidency to Lincoln, Douglas pledged his support to the President-elect, and then travelled south on a strenuous speaking tour to convince southerners that they should remain loyal to the Union. He was booed off the platform in many towns and returned to Washington D.C., exhausted and depressed. In this weakened condition he caught cold, rapidly grew weaker, and died.

Douglas may have been Lincoln's political enemy, but it can be debated whether Lincoln would ever have risen to the heights he did without the constant goading presence of Douglas, seemingly always one step ahead of him in gathering the esteem of his fellow Illinoisans.

***

In July, 1861, the first large scale battle of the war was fought along the banks of Bull Run Creek, about 30 miles southeast of Washington. Both sides hoped that this would be the battle that determined the future of their country. Over 60,000 men were involved, and when it was over, 5,000 men had been killed, wounded or captured, far more than either side had expected. The Union had suffered an embarrassing defeat, and afterward its army had fallen back to Washington D. C. in disarray and confusion. The North was shocked and mortified by the loss.

In late September, Mary Lincoln came down with "chills." She wrote to her cousin Elizabeth Todd Grimsley, "This is my day of rest, so I am sitting up – I am beginning to feel very weak. If they (the chills) cannot be broken in a few days, Mr. Lincoln wants me to go north, and remain until cold weather." Mary recovered slowly, and remained at her husband's side.

After several months of refitting and a change in command, the army was ready to fight again. Major General George McLellan, the new commander of the Union army, ordered a reconnaissance in force of a rebel position on the heights above the Potomac River, at a place called Ball's Bluff. The operation was to take place on October 21st. The day before, **Edward Baker**, Lincoln's old friend and former Congressman from Illinois came to visit the

President at the White House. He wanted to share his excitement with the President that he had received the assignment to lead the probe. Baker and Lincoln sat on the lawn of the Executive Mansion, sharing stories about the old days riding the Eighth Judicial Circuit back in Illinois. Willie Lincoln ran out to greet Baker, and the Colonel lifted him up and gave him a kiss. Mary joined them, bringing Baker some flowers cut fresh from the mansion's green house. They all talked for an hour or more, and then Baker excused himself and rode off to complete preparations for his men's morning march.

The next day, while President Lincoln was visiting General McLellan's headquarters, news came in over the telegraph about the Ball's Bluff operation. A messenger gave the President the news – Baker was dead. His unit had been surprised by a large force of Confederate soldiers after scaling the heights, and they had been severely repulsed by heavy rifle and cannon fire. Baker had been struck in the head by a rifle shot and killed instantly. Mrs. J. Wainwright Ray, who was present at the scene, described the President's reaction as he stumbled out of the headquarters office

...with bowed head, and tears rolling down his cheeks, his face pale and wan, and his heart heaving with emotion.... With both hands pressed upon his heart he walked down the street, not returning the salute of the sentry pacing his beat before the door.[6]

Back at the White House, Lincoln broke the news to Mary and the boys. That night, with a heavy rain beating against the windows of the White House, Lincoln paced back and forth alone in his office, while young Willie Lincoln sat at a writing desk, penning a poem of tribute to their friend. The poem was printed days later in the "Washington National Republican."

There was no patriot like Baker,

So noble and so true:

He fell as a soldier on the field,

His face to the sky of blue.[7]

223

Willie was a serious boy, who enjoyed writing poetry, and memorizing railroad travel timetables. He was thought to be closest in temperament and talents to his father, and both Mary and Abraham took pride in showing off his skills to visitors and friends. Willie and his younger brother Tad were constantly exploring the rooms of the White House together, chasing their pet goat, Nanny, into cabinet meetings, playing pranks on unsuspecting guests, and creating a joyful atmosphere that helped the President bear up under the ever increasing strains of his office.

By the end of 1861, after eight months of war, over 8,000 soldiers of the North and South had been killed, wounded, or declared missing. The slow, steady increase of casualties was falling drop by drop upon the conscience of the President of the United States. He began to have difficulty sleeping, and was seen by his secretaries on many nights, wandering the corridors of the darkened White House in his slippers and night gown.

***

With all the gloomy news of the war bringing down the mood of the nation, Mary Lincoln decided to hold a gathering at the White House, to show the country that its government was continuing to function as normally as possible. The President was skeptical, but in the end agreed. From the very outset, the event was plagued by detractors. Senator Benjamin Wade, President Pro-Tempore of the U.S. Senate, replied to his invitation:

Are the President and Mrs. Lincoln aware that there is a civil war? If they are not, Mr. and Mrs. Wade are, and for that reason decline to participate in dancing and feasting.[8]

When all the invitations had been delivered, half of official Washington was thrilled to have received one, and the other half, who had expected to, but didn't, were furious.

Mary Lincoln almost cancelled the event at the last minute, when eleven year old **Willie Lincoln** came down with a case of "bilious fever." The President suggested that before cancelling the event and disappointing hundreds of people, she should call a doctor in to examine the boy. When Dr. Robert Stone examined Willie, he concluded that the boy was "in no immediate danger," so Abraham and Mary decided to go on with the ball as planned.

During the course of the evening, as band music echoed throughout the mansion, the President and Mrs. Lincoln excused themselves from the ball frequently, and went upstairs to Willie's room, to check on him. The young boy was having difficulty breathing, and his condition seemed to have deteriorated. Days passed and Willie's condition remained poor. Tad, their youngest son, came down with similar symptoms and soon was bedridden as well. President Lincoln continued to attend the constant stream of meetings that punctuated his every day in the White House, stealing away when he could to visit his sons. Mary sat at Willie's side, then Tad's, paralyzed with fear, remembering the days she had spent by the bedside of her three year old son Eddie, helplessly watching him as he slowly slipped away.

Fifteen days after Doctor Stone had declared him in no immediate danger, **William Wallace Lincoln died**. As Elizabeth Keckley, Mrs. Lincoln's seamstress and confidant washed and dressed Willie's body, the President stared down at him saying:

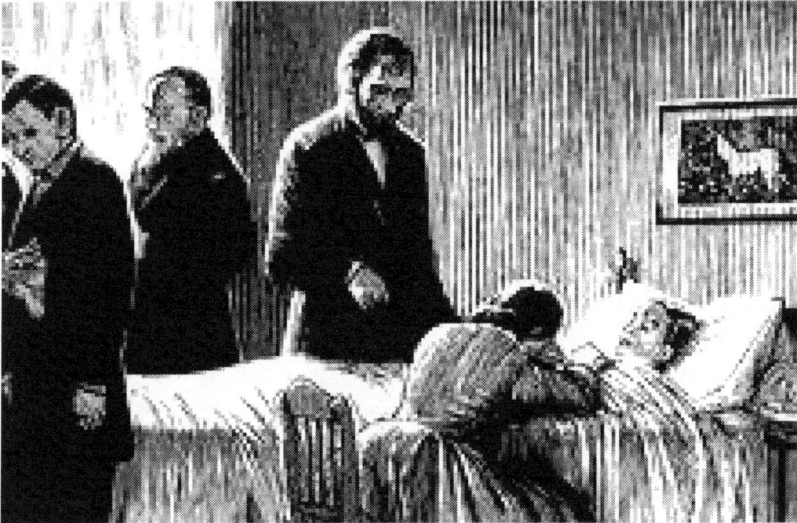

My poor boy, he was too good for this earth. God has called him home. I know that he is much better off in heaven, but then we loved him so. It is hard, hard to have him die. [9]

Mary Lincoln remained in her room, hysterical, wailing and convulsing. She showed all the symptoms of having suffered a nervous breakdown. Tad Lincoln, who had recovered from his illness, was so overcome with grief for his lost brother and companion that he collapsed. Compounding Tad's misery, Mary Lincoln, in her grief, had banned his playmates, Bud and Holly Taft from coming to the White House to console Tad. She feared that seeing the Taft boys would remind her of Willie, and send her into uncontrollable, convulsive wailing. Bud and Holly Taft, who had played with Willie and Tad often since their first days in the White House, would never come there again.

Abraham Lincoln did not have the luxury to grieve so publicly. He had to go on with the work of running a nation during war, regardless of his pain and anguish. But the losses, personal and national, were having an effect. For weeks after Willie's death, the President was prone to bouts of crying on Thursdays, the day Willie had died.

Lincoln had never paid much attention to what he ate, but by 1862, if his wife did not force him to, he would forget to eat much at all. His private secretary, John Hay said that a "good" breakfast for the President was one fried egg, one piece of toast and a cup of coffee. A typical lunch was one biscuit and a glass of milk in the winter and a biscuit, some grapes or other fruit in the summer. Dinner was sometimes eaten as late as midnight, when his day of work ended. In the first year of his Presidency he lost over 40 pounds.

***

In April, 1862, the worst days of the war broke upon the nation. At Shiloh, in Tennessee, near an old white clapboard Dunker church, a great battle was fought. One year earlier, at Bull Run, the nation had been shaken by casualty reports of 5,000 men killed and wounded. After the battle at Shiloh, people across the North gathered in their town squares to read the casualty reports from that battle. Over 24,000 men were killed, wounded, or missing. The nation went into mourning. There were no more hopes of a short war. The South seemed to be winning battles more often than not. People began to question the abilities of their army, and the leadership of their President.

The anguish felt in many homes over divided families, with one son fighting for the Union, another for the Confederacy, was also felt In the White House. Mary Lincoln lost Samuel Todd, her step-brother, at Shiloh, fighting for the Confederacy. Several months later she lost another step-brother, Alex Todd, also fighting for the Confederacy. These losses were especially hard on her. As the wife of the President of the United States, she could not show too much grief publicly over the deaths of soldiers fighting against the Union. She had to confine her mourning for her step-brothers to the family's rooms in the White House. It put a great strain on her already fragile state, as she was still mourning for her son Willie. And her husband was too distracted by his work to be of much comfort to her.

The nation was growing frustrated by ever increasing casualty lists. Many people began to openly speak of compromise with the South, calling on the government to let them go in peace. Others argued that the President should make clear the purpose of all the bloodshed taking place. Up to this point President Lincoln had been unwilling to do anything about slavery in the southern states, seeing that as beyond his Constitution powers. Horace Greely, influential editor of the New York Tribune, published an open letter to the President, which he entitled "The Prayer of Twenty Millions." In it he urged the President to issue a proclamation to free all slaves that were within Union lines, and that might in the future come within those lines. Greeley wanted slavery's extinction to be the focus of the war. Lincoln replied to Greeley:

As to the policy I 'seem to be pursuing,' as you say, I have not meant to leave anyone in doubt.

I would save the Union. I would save it the shortest way under the Constitution...If I could save the Union without freeing any slave, I would do it, and if I could save it by freeing all the slaves, I would do it; and if I could save it by freeing some and leaving others alone, I would also do that. What I do about slavery and the colored race, I do because I believe it helps to save the Union.[10]

By the end of the second year of the Civil War, over 170,000 men had been killed, wounded or declared missing.

***

1863 brought more frustration for the President to deal with. In May, Union forces had been badly defeated at Chancellorsville, Virginia, where a smaller Confederate force surprised and routed a much larger Union army. After the defeat, Robert E. Lee's Army of Northern

Virginia slipped by Union forces and headed north. No one seemed to know where his army was, or where it was headed. President Lincoln relieved the Union commander who had lost at Chancellorsville and replaced him with George Meade, former commander of one of the army's infantry corps. Meade was struggling to learn who his new staff was and how to get a handle on his sprawling command as his army streamed north in search of Lee's troops.

The President made frequent trips alone at night across the broad, tree shaded space between the White House and the War Department, to its **telegraph office,** where all the reports from commanders in the field were received. There he anxiously studied the newest communications, hoping to read that Lee's army had been located. How much danger might the capitol be in? Could Lee out march Meade's troops and seize Washington D. C.? If they succeeded in doing that, then the North might be forced to negotiate peace terms, and the Union would be lost.

The Lincolns were in the habit of spending summer evenings at the Soldier's Home, a property situated on a hill about 3 miles north of the White House. There was a large frame house on the grounds there, cooled by hilltop breezes that could not be felt down in swampy mire of Washington. Lincoln would travel from there each morning either on horseback or by carriage, down to the White House, to attend to his duties, and then return at night. Sometimes he was escorted by a small group of cavalry, sometimes he rode alone. On July 2, 1863, he was anxious to get to his office to read the latest dispatches from the field. Units of Lee's army had struck a small brigade of Union cavalry in the crossroads town of Gettysburg, Pennsylvania. A fight had commenced July 1st that might develop into something significant. Lincoln decide to forgo riding to the White House in his carriage with Mary, and instead mounted his horse, Old Bob, and took off with a small group of bodyguards, telling Mary to take his carriage and join him later.

Not long after he arrived at the White House, Lincoln got news that Mrs. Lincoln had been injured in an accident as she was being driven from the Soldiers Home to the White House. The driver's seat of the carriage came loose, throwing the driver off the vehicle. This startled the horses, and they bolted, beginning to run wildly down the road with only the frightened Mary aboard. She quickly realized the danger she was in, and jumped free. When she hit the ground her head struck a rock and was deeply gashed. Her escort took her to a nearby hospital, where doctors bandaged her head and checked her thoroughly for any other injuries. The President was assured that she was doing well, and that a quick recovery was expected.

An investigation of the President's carriage later revealed that someone had loosened the bolts that attached the driver's seat to the carriage frame. The President had been expected to use the carriage that morning, and it now appeared that Mary's injury was a result of a deliberate attempt to injure the President. He dismissed that conclusion as unlikely.

Years later Robert Lincoln was reported to have said that Mary never fully recovered from the accident. Her migraines became more frequent, eventually accompanied by hallucinations.

***

As Lincoln worried over his wife's recovery, the battle at Gettysburg grew into the largest conflict of the war. Over three days in the farm fields of Pennsylvania, over 75,000 Confederate and 90,000 Union soldiers fought viciously, many times hand-to-hand, to gain victory. Robert E. Lee's troops failed to dislodge Meade's army from the heights below the town, and retreated back to Virginia. Final casualty reports for both armies topped 51,000 men.

A day later, in Mississippi, Ulysses S. Grant's Union army captured the Confederate stronghold at Vicksburg, Mississippi, opening up the Mississippi River to Union gunboats that could now travel unmolested all the way down to New Orleans. The Lincoln's learned that same day that Mary had lost another step-brother, David Todd, who had been killed in the battle.

With the twin military victories at Gettysburg and Vicksburg, the White House should have been filled with joyful celebration, but Mary's injury and more family loss made celebration impossible, and those family losses were not yet over.

In September, 1863, **Benjamin Hardin Helm**, a General in the Confederate Army, was killed at the battle of Chickamauga, in Tennessee. President Lincoln had offered Helm, who was married to Mary Lincoln's favorite sister, Emilie, a high position in the Union army at the beginning of the war, but Helm had turned him down, preferring to fight for the South. Both of the Lincolns were deeply affected by Helm's death. The young girl whom the President affectionately called "Little Sister," was now a widow. The Lincoln's were no stranger to the sorrow felt by so many other families who had suffered loss during the war.

The Lincolns brought **Emilie Helm** through the lines with a note from the President offering her safe passage to the White House. They hoped to console her in her time of need and loss. But this kind move brought criticism to the Lincolns from their enemies in the press. Mary was accused of harboring a traitor, and of sharing military secrets with her southern kin. Emilie wrote after the war that one evening, after reading some of these stinging stories in the newspaper, Mary dropped the pages, held out her arms to her sister, hugged her hard and said, "Oh, Emilie, will we ever awake from this hideous nightmare?"[11]

By the end of the third year of the Civil War, almost 350,000 Americans had been killed, wounded or captured. No President in the nation's history had ever presided over such a bloodbath. The entire South and a good portion of the people of the North saw Abraham Lincoln as a butcher of unparalleled savagery.

***

The war ground on. After Gettysburg, Lee's army had trouble replacing its many casualties, and as it grew weaker, Lee adopted a defensive strategy. He would fight from fixed positions, and defend southern ground as stubbornly as possible, going on the offense only if the promise of success was high. The new commander of all Union forces, General Ulysses Grant, led a huge army south, intending to attack Lee relentlessly, until the South had no more men fit to bear arms. President Lincoln had finally found a commander that believed what he did: that the Union, with far greater industrial capability and far greater manpower, could eventually grind down the South, so long as Northern will did not falter. It was a strategy that meant terrible casualties, but inevitable victory.

In the summer of 1864, the South launched its last invasion of the north. A small army led by General Jubal Early slipped away from a Union force that was supposed to keep it bottled up in the Shenandoah Valley of Virginia, and marched toward Washington D. C. Early knew he did not have the troop strength to seize Washington, for since the early months of the war the capitol had been ringed with a string of powerful earthworks and forts. Early did hope to draw enough troops away from Ulysses Grant's Union army, which was laying siege to the Confederate capitol in Richmond, to give Robert E. Lee's defending force an opportunity to strike a blow against their much larger opponent. Early marched his men hard, and reached the outskirts of Washington D. C. before Union reinforcements from Grant's army arrived.

On July, 11, 1864, he prepared an assault on an earthwork known as **Fort Stevens**, just a few miles north of the White House. President Lincoln, who was summering at the Soldiers Home with Mary and Tad, had been informed that rebel forces were quite close, and that an attack was imminent. The President urged Mary to take Tad with her back to the White House, where they might be more secure. Mary refused, and when she learned that her husband was headed to Fort Stevens to observe the Confederate troops gathered near there, she insisted on coming with him. When the President and First Lady arrived, they were lead up to the top ramp of the fortification, where an officer pointed out to them the location of the rebel troops. Lincoln was wearing his distinctive, tall, stovepipe hat, and must have made an irresistible target for a Confederate sharpshooter who was situated on the roof of a house three hundred yards away. A soldier stationed at the fort later wrote to his wife about what happened next:

Old Abe and his wife was in the fort at the time and Old Abe and his doctor was standing up on the parapets and the sharpshooter shot the doctor through the left thigh, and Old Abe ordered our men to fall back.[12]

As the troops fell back, the President lingered for a moment, and then a nearby officer (Oliver Wendell Holmes, who after the war became a Justice of the Supreme Court), yelled out to him, "Get down, you damned fool!" The President reluctantly complied. Mary Lincoln, knowing that the Confederates might launch an all-out assault at any moment, pleaded with the President to leave the fort, but he instead remained for some time, greeting and thanking the troops there for their devotion to the Union. Reinforcements from General Grant's army arrived by boat at the docks in Washington within the hour, and Confederate General Jubal Early's men were forced to retreat back to Virginia. No Confederate armed force would ever again approach the U. S. capital.

***

The public was sick of war. Though Lincoln had by now been re-nominated by the Republican Party for another term as President, few thought he would be elected. Over a year earlier, Lincoln had signed the Emancipation Proclamation, and in doing so had shifted the reason for the war from Union at any cost, to Union without slavery. Thurlow Weed, boss of New York Republican politics, wrote Lincoln that his election was "an impossibility." Weed went on to say "The people are wild for Peace. They are told that the President will only listen to terms of Peace on condition Slavery be abandoned." Horace Greeley, editor of the New York Tribune, wanted to find someone to replace Lincoln as the Republican standard bearer. Lincoln's Illinois friend, Orville H. Browning, wrote to a colleague, explaining that he believed it was all over, that he had never expected much from his old friend Lincoln. "I thought he might get through, as many a boy has got through college, without disgrace and without knowledge, but I fear he is a failure." [13]

The President himself felt like he had failed. To paraphrase Lincoln, the bottom seems to have come out of the tub. Northern morale was at a low point, their armies stalemated. Grant's Army of the Potomac had been fighting its way south through Virginia incurring the worst casualties of the war, yet Richmond, the Confederate capital, still seemed unreachable. Out west, General William T. Sherman's Army of Tennessee had been laying siege to Atlanta, Georgia, the key to the South's weakly defended interior, without success. In late August, the President wrote a letter to his cabinet and filed it away, to be opened and read to them in the event he was defeated for re-election.

This morning as for some days, it seems exceedingly probable that this Administration will not be re-elected. Then it will be my duty to so co-operate with the President-elect, as to save the Union between the election and the inauguration; as he will have secured his election on such ground that he cannot possibly save it afterwards. [14]

***

The Lincoln family had been spending the summer of 1864 at the **Anderson Cottage on the grounds of the Soldier's Home,** as was their custom, when the heat of

Washington's summer became unbearable and the mosquito population exploded. President Lincoln left each morning to ride on horseback or by carriage, down to the White House to complete his day of meetings before returning home. Frequently he rode alone, as Presidential security had not yet become an issue.

One evening in August, while returning home alone to the Soldier's Home, **Lincoln's horse, Old Bob**, was startled by a loud crack, and bolted down the road at breakneck speed. The President struggled and was able to regain control of the animal just as he reached the grounds of the Soldier's Home. Lincoln noticed that he had lost his stovepipe hat during the wild ride, and asked an officer to send a soldier back down the road to retrieve it. Sometime later the soldier showed up and presented Lincoln with the hat. There was a hole in it, just above the hatband. Apparently, a bullet had passed clean through it, just above the top of the President's head. Lincoln laughed it off as an errant bullet fired by a hunter somewhere in the woods. Secretary of War Stanton increased Lincoln's guard and insisted that in the future he not ride alone from the White House to the Old Soldier's Home.[15]

Lincoln was adamant about keeping security measures to a minimum. "It would never do for a President to have guards with drawn swords at his door, as if he were, or fancied he were, or were trying to be, or were assuming to be an emperor." He thought that if someone really wanted to hurt him, that person could not be stopped. "A conspiracy to assassinate, if such there were, could easily obtain a pass to see me for any one or more of its instruments."[16]

When the Secretary of the Senate, John. W. Forney visited him at the White House, the President showed him a pigeonhole in his desk that was stuffed with over 80 letters. All were threats of kidnapping and death that had been thought serious enough not to be thrown out, as most were. "I know I am in danger," he told Forney, "but I am not going to worry over threats like these."

What was not known until after the war was that in September, 1864, a sometime preacher and confederate spy named **T.N. Conrad**, had infiltrated Union lines with three others, with the intention of kidnapping the President. Their plan had been to seize the President during one of his solitary rides from the Old Soldiers Home to the White House, but the plot was foiled when Conrad discovered that Lincoln was accompanied by a troop of cavalry on the day they were to make their attempt. Luck had been with the President that day. Conrad and his men did not depart Washington D.C. until November, hoping to get another chance at the President. They failed.

With casualty rates soaring, armies stalemated, re-election in doubt, and a tide of death threats flowing in, it is not hard to imagine that Lincoln was having difficulty sleeping and keeping up his health and spirits as the November elections drew near.

Just when all seemed as dark as it could get, a ray of sunlight broke through the gloom. Lincoln received a telegraph message at the war department, from General Sherman in Georgia. On September 2nd, 1864, Atlanta had finally surrendered to Union troops. The way was now open for Sherman's army to attack deep into the very heart of the Confederacy. Morale around the country spiked upward. For the first time since the beginning of the war, people could see that there was a path to victory.

In November, President Lincoln was re-elected He would have four more years to make the Union whole again, and heal its wounds. Before he could begin to consider other goals for his next term, one in which he would govern a nation at peace, there were still battles to fight, both in the field and in Congress. In a message to the lame duck session of the Thirty-Eighth Congress, the President urged members to take heed of the mood of the country as reflected in the returns of the past election, and reconsider passing an amendment to the Constitution banning the institution of slavery. The amendment had been defeated before, but now the President actively joined the effort to secure its passage. Doris Kearns Goodwin, in her book, Team of Rivals, told the story beautifully, and Steven Spielberg's movie LINCOLN brought the story to life in a moving way. By January 31, 1865, Congress passed the amendment, and sent it out to the states for ratification (which would be achieved by December, 1865).

Lincoln had told his friends many times in his youth that he will have lived in vain if he did not leave some mark on the country before his passing. Now he had made his mark. Slavery, the institution that he felt kept America from securing its moral superiority over the other nations of the world, was gone.

As the fourth year of the Civil War came to a close, 485, 840 Americans had been killed, wounded or captured. The country was awash in blood, and families all over the north and south were continuing to receive letters telling them their loved ones were never coming home.

One such letter was received by Lydia Bixby of Massachusetts, written to her by President Lincoln. The sentiments in it are as fresh and applicable to today's gold star mothers as they were to her back then:

Dear Madam,

I have been shown in the files of the War Department, a statement of the Adjutant General of Massachusetts, that you are the mother of five sons who have died gloriously on the field of battle.

I feel how weak and fruitless must be any words of mine which should attempt to beguile you from the grief of a loss so overwhelming. But I cannot refrain from tendering to you the consolation that may be found in the thanks of the republic they died to save.

I pray that our heavenly father may assuage the anguish of your bereavement, and leave you only the cherished memory of the loved and lost, and the solemn pride that must be yours to have laid so costly a sacrifice upon the altar of freedom. Yours very respectfully and sincerely,

A. Lincoln[17]

***

In January, 1865, Attorney General James Speed, brother of Lincoln's closest friend, Joshua, visited with the President at the White House. He had not seen Lincoln for several years before his appointment to the cabinet, and he was shocked at how careworn, pale and thin the President looked. When Speed mentioned to the President his dismay over how many pardons the President was awarding to soldiers in the field, Lincoln rose quickly to reply, and fainted. Dr. Stone, his physician in the White House, ordered the President to stay in bed for the next 24 hours.

A month later Senator Orville Browning reported on a visit he paid to the President. "The President", he said, "looked badly and felt badly – apparently more depressed than I have seen him since he became President."

Soon after Browning's visit, Joshua Speed came from his home in Kentucky to see the President. Speed related the content of his meeting with Lincoln to William Herndon in an 1866 letter. Lincoln had been meeting with two ladies who requested that he have their husbands released from jail, where they were serving time for resisting the draft. After considering the matter briefly he said to the women, "Well...these fellows have suffered long enough and I have thought so for some time and now that mind is on it again, I believe I will turn out the flock," whereupon he issued orders for their release. The overjoyed ladies thanked him and departed. Speed then said to the President, "Lincoln, with my knowledge of your nervous sensibility it is a wonder that such scenes as this don't kill you." Lincoln replied, "I am very unwell, my feet and hands are always cold – I suppose I ought to be in bed....Speed, die when I may I want it said of me by those who know me best to say that I always plucked a thistle and planted a flower where I thought a flower would grow."[18] That was the last time the two old friends saw each other.

Preparations were being made at the capitol building for the second inauguration. General Sherman's army was marching through Georgia, meeting little opposition. Soon he would reach the Atlantic Ocean, cutting the Confederacy in two. Grant's huge army was still laying siege to Richmond and Petersburg, Virginia, and it seemed only a matter of time before the capitol of the Confederacy fell. Huge casualty lists were being posted all over the North and South, and while the end was in sight, families around the nation were continuing to hang black crepe on their fireplace mantles to mourn their lost members.

The President was continuing to feel unwell, so Mary sent for some "blue pills" (calomel), from a close by pharmacy, to ease Lincoln's condition. After taking the pills and spending a restless night, Lincoln awoke white as a sheet, unable to get out of bed. Mary insisted that the President remain in bed until he felt stronger. After two days he recovered his strength. Both Abraham and Mary thought it strange that the pills, which he had taken before, had affected him as they did, but merely concluded that the pharmacist had not made up the prescription properly. They agreed not to use that pharmacy again. Only after Lincoln's death was it discovered that David Herold (who later would be involved in the Lincoln assassination) worked at that pharmacy. After the war, in a letter to a friend, Jane Swisshelm, Mary speculated that her husband might have been poisoned.[19]

On March fourth, the day of **Lincoln's second inauguration**, victory was in the air. The armies of the Union were advancing on all fronts, and Washington's population was ready to hear the President condemn his enemies for the misery they had brought, and heap praise on their own triumphant forces. The weather was not in keeping with the joyous mood of the crowd. It had rained all morning, and forced the inaugural ceremonies to begin indoors. Andrew Johnson, who appeared intoxicated, gave a rambling, nearly incoherent speech after being sworn in as Vice-President. Lincoln was mortified, and thankful that the weather had kept Johnson from addressing the much larger crowd that still waited outside in the rain, hoping to see the President. The steady rain let up, and the decision was made to move the Presidential address back outdoors.

As the President was introduced to the crowd of some thirty thousand, they began a steady roar of cheers and applause that kept up even as Lincoln tried to get them to stop. Finally he succeeded, and as the crowd became silent, the clouds, which had been thick, dark and threatening all morning, suddenly parted, and a bright shaft of sunlight broke through and illuminated the President as he began to speak. Everyone in the crowd took notice of this, and most considered it a heaven sent omen of good things to come. In that crowd, looking down on the President from just 20 feet away, was **John Wilkes Booth**. Careful study of a photographic enlargement of the scene, done years later, revealed his presence.

Lincoln spoke in a slow, deliberate manner. He did not excoriate the South. He did not praise the North. He laid blame for the bloody four year conflict on both sides, saying "...one of them would make war rather than let the nation survive, and the other would rather accept war rather than let it perish. And the war came." This was not the speech the people had expected to hear from their victorious chief.

"Both", he continued, "read the same bible, and pray to the same God, and each invokes His aid against the other. The prayers of both could not be answered; that of neither has been answered fully. The Almighty has his own purposes."

He went on to say that slavery was an offence against God, and that God willed to remove it, punishing both sides with a Civil War "as a woe due to those by whom the offence came."

When would the war end? "Fondly do we hope, fervently do we pray that this mighty scourge of war may speedily pass away. Yet if God wills that it continue...the judgements of the Lord are true and righteous altogether (Ps. 19.9)." The end would come when God decided each side had suffered enough for their offence.

In his closing remarks, Lincoln asked the people to submit to the will of God, and do only what was in their power to do.

With malice toward none, with charity for all; with firmness in the right as God gives us to see the right, let us strive on to finish the work we are in; to bind up the nation's wounds; to care for him who shall have borne the battle, and for his widow and orphan – to do all which may achieve and cherish a just and lasting peace, among ourselves, and with all nations."[20]

Days after the speech, Lincoln wrote to Thurlow Weed in New York, assessing his address. "I expect the latter (the address) to wear as well as - perhaps better than anything I have produced; but I believe it is not immediately popular. Men are not flattered by being shown that there has been a difference of purpose between the Almighty and them."

On April 2, 1865, General Robert E. Lee ordered his greatly reduced army to abandon the trenches around Richmond and Petersburg, Virginia. They would march west and try to regroup before Ulysses Grant's forces could overwhelm them. Two days later, Abraham Lincoln arrived by steamer at the docks of Richmond, Virginia, and stepped onto the land the South had fought so long to defend. He headed up deserted streets with a small guard of Navy men, to the Confederate White House, where only days before, Jefferson Davis, President of the Confederacy, had been holding meetings with his cabinet. Hundreds of black people, now freed from their bondage, flocked about him as Lincoln climbed the stairs, entered Davis' executive mansion, and settled into the chair in Jefferson Davis' office. After over 600,000 casualties, the war was nearly over.

***

When President Lincoln returned to Washington, he told Mary and a gathering of friends of strange dreams that had been making sleep difficult for him in the past few days. He related how he awoke from one such dream and picked up his bedside Bible, looking for verses to comfort him, when his eyes fell upon passages that spoke of dreams, visions and supernatural visitations. "You frighten me!" Mary exclaimed. "What is the matter?"

Lincoln then told the group of his most recent dream.

About ten days ago I retired very late. I had been up waiting for important dispatches from the front. I could not have been long in bed when I fell into a slumber, for I was weary. I soon began to dream. There seemed to be a death-like stillness about me. Then I heard subdued sobs, as if a number of people were weeping. I thought I left my bed and wandered downstairs. There the silence was broken by the same pitiful sobbing, but the mourners were invisible. I went from room to room; no living person was in sight, but the same mournful sounds of distress met me as I passed along. It was light in all the rooms; every object was familiar to me; but where were all the people who were grieving as if their hearts would break? I was puzzled and alarmed. What could be the meaning of all this? Determined to find the cause of a state of things so mysterious and shocking, I kept on until I arrived at the East Room, which I entered. There I met with a sickening surprise. Before me was a catafalque, on which rested a corpse wrapped in funeral vestments. Around it were stationed soldiers who were acting as guards, and there was a throng of people, some gazing mournfully upon the corpse, whose face was covered, others weeping pitifully. 'Who is dead in the White House?' I demanded of one of the soldiers. 'The President,' was his answer; he was killed by an assassin.' Then came a loud burst of grief from the crowd.[21]

Ward Hill Lamon, who was present when Lincoln told the story, remembered the President to be "grave, gloomy and at times visibly pale" as he spoke. Mary was very upset by it, and said to her husband, "That is horrid. I wish you had not told it!" "Well," Lincoln replied, "it is only a dream, Mary. Let us say no more about it, and try to forget it."[22]

Three days later, Union forces encircled the Army of Northern Virginia, the South's best fighting force still in the field, near Appomattox Court House in Virginia, and forced it to surrender. More Southern forces remained active in the Carolinas, Arkansas and Texas, but this surrender meant the Civil War was effectively over. People filled the streets of Washington D. C. long into the night, whooping, cheering, lighting off fireworks and firing guns into the air. The nightmare of daily casualty lists would finally stop, and the President and the people of the country could begin to plan for a future at peace.

***

April 14th dawned dreary, dark and wet, with a shroud-like, misty fog hanging over the city. Lincoln had a busy day planned; meetings with citizens petitioning for various jobs, pardons, and favors; then a cabinet meeting, and later a relaxing carriage ride with Mary. The day would end with an evening at the theatre, along with General Grant and his wife, Julia. People wanted to see the man they had begun calling Father Abraham, and the General who had finally gotten the best of Robert E. Lee.

The cabinet meeting convened at the 11am. There was much to discuss. General Grant was in attendance, and the President was eager to hear from him the details of Lee's surrender at Appomattox. Grant explained to the group:

245

I told them to go back to their homes and families, and they would not be molested, if they did nothing more.[23]

At a meeting held with Generals Grant and Sherman aboard the River Queen while it was docked near Richmond, Lincoln had instructed his Generals to "let 'em up easy." Lincoln was pleased to hear that Grant had done just that with Lee's Army, allowing them to take with them a personal side arm, and a horse, if they owned one. This would assist them in defending their homes and working their farms as they returned to the Union as citizens.

Lincoln then told his cabinet of yet another dream he had had recently, one that he had experienced before. Secretary of the Navy Gideon Welles wrote about it in his diary:

Generally, the news had been favorable which succeeded this dream, and the dream itself was always the same...He said it related to the water; that he seemed to be in some singular, indescribable vessel, and that he was moving with great rapidity toward an indefinite shore...

Then, the President continued, "*I had this same dream again last night, and we shall, judging from the past, have great news very soon.*"[24]

On their carriage ride that afternoon, the President told Mary that they had been sad for so long, that they had to resolve to be happier. Once he finished his second term, he thought they might go abroad and visit the Holy Land. After that, he wanted to go back to Springfield, dust off his Lincoln and Herndon sign, and practice law. Eventually they might buy a little prairie farm on the banks of the Sangamon River. "I never felt so happy in my life," he told her.

After the ride was done, there were a few more meetings, and then the couple changed for a night at the theatre. General Grant and his wife had declined the President's invitation to attend, claiming they were eager to get home to their children. In truth, Julia Grant greatly disliked Mary Lincoln, who had treated her rudely in past meetings. A few other couples also refused the invitation, citing fatigue or previous commitments. At the last minute, the Lincoln's sent an invitation to

Miss Clara Harris, daughter of a Senator from Iowa, and frequent guest of Mrs. Lincoln. Clara was thrilled to accept for herself and her fiancé, Major Henry Rathbone.

As he left the White House at 8pm that night, Lincoln, already running late for the performance at Ford's Theater, said goodbye to the butler, who thought it strange, as the President always bid him good night.

Two hours later, Abraham Lincoln, 16th President of the United States, who had been haunted his entire life by death, through dreams and personal tragedies, lay motionless and silent, slowly bleeding his life away in a strange bed in a strange room far from the prairies of Illinois he loved so well, a victim of an assassin's bullet.

William Kolasinski

Chapter Fourteen

DEALING WITH THE DARKNESS

I n his book, "Lincoln's Battle with God," Stephen Mansfield described Abraham Lincoln as "a man who beat back the spirits that came for him in the night."[1] Just how did a man so beset by death, suffering and loss that he frequently contemplated suicide, not only survive, but transform himself into the leader that guided our nation through the bloodiest, most traumatic period in its history? We cannot finally understand the man without understanding how he managed this remarkable feat.

***

As a boy from a family of very modest means, living in a rural community, Lincoln must have felt his options were being limited by fate. The harshness of his living conditions and the endless life of hard work that he faced could either break his spirit or inspire him to overcome what seemed to be his inevitable lot. Consciously or not, he chose the latter.

When he was no more than eight years old in Kentucky, he was already known in the community as someone who could read better than most adults in the community, and was called on to write letters for many of his neighbors who were illiterate. He found reading a means of broadening his knowledge and a means of escape from the monotony of everyday frontier life. Dennis Hanks, a relative and close friend of Lincoln's when he was growing up in Indiana, listed several of the books Lincoln had read between ages nine and sixteen. They included Defoe's "Robinson Crusoe," Bunyan's "Pilgrim's Progress," Mason Weems "Life of Washington," "Sinbad the Sailor," and "Aesop's Fables." He was known to carry a copy of the latter in his saddlebag as an adult. These writings opened up a world of adventure to young Lincoln, and taught him lessons about how honesty and hard work could move a man ahead in life. The more he read, the more he set himself apart from those around him, gaining their respect as a valuable member of his frontier community. This fueled his desire to read and learn as much as he could, given his limited free time and even more limited resources. Reading remained a passion and a pleasure for him throughout his life. As he grew older and experienced more and more pain and frustration through the death of loved ones, business failures, mounting debts and lost loves, reading helped him to cope, providing entertainment and escape, if only for hours at a time.

Soon after he discovered the joy of reading, Lincoln began to develop a skill he learned from observing his father, Thomas. Thomas was known as a **master story teller**, and Abraham frequently observed how a crowd would gather around Thomas as he began one of his yarns. From his earliest days as an adult, Abraham's neighbors and friends commented on how he seemed to have an endless store of jokes and stories to quote for any occasion. Many described the remarkable transformation he underwent when he began to tell a joke or story. His naturally sad demeanor would quickly fade as his eyes

widened, then crinkled into slits. His voice would mimic an appropriate accent, whether it was a backwoods Kentucky twang or a Scotch or Irish brogue. As he came nearer to the finish of the tale, his usually taut lips would lift into a broad grin; his face would crease with deep laugh lines, and he would quickly exhale a loud guffaw and slap his hand on his knee. He told jokes and stories to make a point, to entertain his listeners, and to lift his own spirits. In his young adulthood, humor became a frequently used medicine to remedy his low spirits. His closest friend, Joshua Speed, said of him:

His worldwide reputation for telling anecdotes – and telling them so well – was in my judgement necessary to his very existence. Most men who have been great students such as he was, in their hours of idleness, have taken to the bottle, to cards or dice. He had no fondness for any of these. Hence he sought relaxation in anecdotes.[2]

David Davis, a judge on the Eighth Judicial Circuit who spent many days and nights listening to Lincoln swap stories and jokes with fellow lawyers and jurists, concluded:

It was wit and joke meeting and loving wit and joke – not the man for the men. Lincoln used these men merely to whistle off sadness- gloom and unhappiness... He used such men as a tool – a thing to satisfy him....[3]

***

Here are just a handful of the stories and jokes that Lincoln was known to have used to great effect.

A political opponent in Kentucky, after seeing Lincoln give a speech, insulted him by saying that when he first heard that Lincoln was a candidate for office he had expected to see a smart looking man. Lincoln laughed off the comment, but, noticing that a friend of his was angry at the remark, he told him this story.

A toper named Bill got brutally drunk and staggered down a narrow alley where he lay himself down in the mud and remained there until the dusk of evening, at which time he recovered from his stupor, and finding himself very muddy, immediately started for a pump to wash himself. On his way to the pump another drunken man was leaning over a horse post. This Bill mistook for the pump and at once took hold of the arm of the man for the handle, the use of which got the occupant of the post to throwing up. Bill, believing all was right put both hands under and gave himself a thorough washing. He then made his way to the grocery for something to drink. On entering the door one of his comrades exclaimed in a tone of surprise. Why Bill, what in the world is the matter? Bill said in reply, you ought to have seen me before I washed up.[4]

*

During the Civil War, General George McLellan, commanding a large Union army, failed to defeat a much smaller rebel army facing him. McLellan had a very high opinion of himself, always dressed immaculately in the finest uniform, and rode at the head of his troops on a coal black charger. After the battle, Lincoln remarked to his aides that McLellan reminded him of Bap McNabb's Little Red Rooster. He then told them this story.

In early times the boys in and about old Sangamon Town got up a free chicken fight...Well, Bap McNabb had a very splendid red rooster, and he, with others, was entered.

The eventful day arrived and Bap with his little beauty was there in all his splendor.

The time arrives and into the ring they toss their chickens, Bap's along with the rest. But no sooner had the little beauty discovered what was to be done, he dropped his tail and run.

Bap, being very much disappointed, picked him up and went home.

As soon as he got home he tossed his pet down in the yard... The little fellow then stood up and flirted out his beautiful feathers and crowed as brave as a lion. Bap viewed this closely and remarked; yes, you little cuss, you are great on a parade, but you are not worth a damn in a fight.[5]

*

When a customer at his store in New Salem commented on his homeliness, he responded with this story:

An extremely ugly man was walking on a narrow road. A woman came by and examined him closely. 'You', she said, 'are the ugliest man I ever saw.' Sadly, the man answered, 'Perhaps so, but I can't help that.' 'No', the woman allowed, 'but you might stay at home.'[6]

*

Lincoln was staying overnight at an inn somewhere on the judicial circuit in rural Illinois when a fellow lawyer split his pants. The other lawyers in the group began to rib the poor fellow, circulating a sheet of paper soliciting donations to buy the lawyer a new pair of pants. They each wrote down their names and a pledge of money. When the paper came to Lincoln he wrote "I can contribute nothing to the end in view."[7]

*

Once, when he was out in a field splitting rails, a man with a gun approached him and called out for Lincoln to look up. When Lincoln did, the man then started to raise his gun, as if he intended to shoot him. Lincoln asked him what he was doing. The man replied that he had promised to shoot the first man he met who was uglier than he was. Lincoln stared at him for a second and said, "If I am uglier than you, then blaze away!"[8]

From young adulthood, Lincoln looked to humor to elevate his spirits. In the White House he frequently surprised official and personal guests by reading from the latest writings of humorist David Ross Locke. Locke created a character named Petroleum V. Nasby, and it is through Nasby's observations and experiences that Locke commented on Civil War times. Lincoln loved Locke's use of vernacular and read Nasby's comments aloud in a thick Irish brogue.

George Vaillant, a psychologist who specializes in adaptations and strategies used to combat depression or anxiety, singled out humor as the best method to minimize the frequency of occurrence and duration of those debilitating states. More by design than accident, Abraham Lincoln benefitted from that strategy.

***

Once Abraham Lincoln reached the age of 21 and left his family's homestead to begin living on his own, he began to formulate a philosophy that would govern the rest of his life. He had been brought up by parents who were hard-shell Baptists. They believed in a righteous God that visited misfortune on people as a punishment for their transgressions. When Lincoln settled in New Salem, Illinois, he joined the local debating society, where discussions about philosophy, God and organized religion took place with regularity. Lincoln was influenced by what he heard from the better educated men of his town, who held no great affection for organized religion or an unforgiving, punishing God. He adopted a philosophy often called predeterminism. Mary Lincoln described it to William Herndon in an 1866 interview;

Mr. Lincoln's maxim and philosophy were – 'What is to be will be and no care of ours can arrest the decree.[9]

One of Lincoln's favorite quotes from Shakespeare, whose tragedies he especially enjoyed, was from Julius Caesar; "There's a divinity that shapes our ends, rough- hew them as we will."

William Herndon recalled that Lincoln did not believe in free will, but rather saw man as a mere tool, a cog in the wheel of a great machine that "strikes and cuts, grinds and mashes, all things, including man, who resist it."

This philosophy allowed Lincoln to accept the hardships he was enduring as part of a plan bigger than his own life, fitting his personal hopes and ambitions into that bigger plan as best he could. He also chose to explain all the pain and suffering that came his way as a tool that would help him improve himself. He explained to William Herndon that "suffering was medicinal and educational."[10] He would learn from it, and grow stronger.

Lincoln adopted a philosophy that depersonalized the negative experiences of his life, and accepted them as a positive that could make him emotionally stronger and intellectually sharper.

This philosophy would allow him to survive the great stresses he faced in his personal life and in holding the country together over the course of the Civil War.

***

While he believed he could not alter his preordained fate in any major way, Lincoln believed there was a way to glimpse the future. He, like many people of his day who grew up on the frontier, believed in signs, omens and dreams. He told John Hay, his Presidential secretary, "I believe I feel trouble in the air before it comes."[11]

His Springfield housekeeper, Maria Vance, in an oral history, quoted her employer as saying,

Visions are not uncommon to me. Nor were they uncommon to that blessed mother of mine...She often spoke of things that would happen, and even foretold her early death.[12]

In 1858, during his Senate debates with Stephen Douglas, Lincoln confided to William Herndon, "I feel as if I should meet a terrible end."[13]

Other of his most famous dreams were detailed in earlier chapters of this book. His "Two Faces in the Mirror Dream", in 1860; his "Fire at the White House Dream" in 1864; his "Ship Travelling to an Unseen Shore Dream", and his "Someone Has Killed the President Dream" in 1865, each caused him to ponder what they were meant to reveal about his future.

He believed that such dreams were windows into a future he must eventually face, and that as such they allowed him to prepare mentally for what was to come.

***

The medical world of his day also provided Lincoln with short term means of dealing with his dark moods. Sometime in the 1850's he began to take a pill called "blue mass." It was a druggist concoction believed to relieve headaches, depression and intestinal difficulties. The pill was made up of calomel (a mercury preparation) and various binding agents. Modern researchers tested these blue mass pills and found that they contained 9,000 times the amount of mercury now considered safe for a person to ingest. Some medical experts have hypothesized that Lincoln may, as a result of using blue mass pills, have suffered from low level Mercury poisoning. They point to reports in the 1850's of Lincoln's outbursts of rage, insomnia, forgetfulness, hands that trembled while he was stressed, and development of a peculiar flat-footed gait, as symptoms of that condition. Lincoln stopped using the blue mass pills before departing Springfield for the White House in 1861, telling his friend John T. Stuart that they made him cross. Most of his symptoms, except his stork like flat-footed gait, then disappeared.[14]

How Lincoln chose to treat, or mistreat, his body affected his emotional balance as well. John Hay, Lincoln's private secretary, said that the President ate irregularly while in the White House. Breakfast, taken around 9am, usually consisted of one fried egg, toast and coffee, if Mary was present to convince him to take the time. Lunch and dinner depended on his workload, and frequently were delayed or skipped entirely. Apples served as a substitute. He ate them daily. Hay said of his eating habits that Lincoln "was very abstemious – ate less than anyone I know. Drank nothing but water – not from principle, but because he did not like wine or spirits." This inconsistency of diet undoubtedly affected his mood and energy level.

***

In his youth Lincoln was well known for his ability to outwrestle and outrun most of the men in his community. Indeed, his physical prowess was one of the attributes that gained him early respect and recognition amongst his neighbors. It may not be surprising then, to learn that Lincoln loved to participate in sports, even into his adult years.

Unlike today, there were few organized activities for athletes to develop and display their skills in the 1800's. Still, Lincoln found many ways to exercise. During his New Salem years he regularly took up challenges to his status as local champion by competing against his neighbors and friends wrestling, running and swimming, whenever he was not busy splitting rails. As an attorney in Springfield he could often be found in the alley behind his law office playing corner ball (an early version of handball). Out on the circuit he competed in log rolling competitions, town ball (an early version of baseball), pitching quoits, and fives (an early form of bowling).

During his years as President, Lincoln, then in his 50's, would occasionally humor guests who asked him to demonstrate his strength. He would do this by holding a heavy chopping axe in each hand at the very end of their handles, slowly raising them up in front of him, and holding them straight out. It never failed to impress the onlookers.

***

In adulthood, Lincoln also found relief from his dark moods in reading poetry and the works of William Shakespeare. His favorite works were those that dwelled on mortality and death. He loved William Knox's poem *Oh, Why Should the Spirit of Mortals Be Proud*, and often recited parts of it to visitors at his Springfield law offices and in the White House. *Macbeth* and *Hamlet* were also such favorites that he had committed large sections to memory, and would often recite stanzas to his cabinet during meetings, much to their dismay. The knowledge that others had suffered as he was suffering gave him some solace.

He wrote his own poetry, beginning at age eight or nine. He scribbled the following in his copybook while growing up in Kentucky:

Abraham Lincoln

His hand and pen

He will be good

But God knows when

By adulthood he was seriously trying to craft poetry that he could be proud of, and that would be good enough to publish. In earlier chapters I quoted at length from his piece about a visit to his boyhood home in Indiana. It is a dark piece, full of the imagery of death, and the fleeting nature of life. Even in his poetry he seemed to come back to the subject of death.

Lincoln kept his darker side at bay with literature, humor, writing and physical activity. He accepted career setbacks and the loss of loved ones as learning experiences that were not unique to him, but typical of universal human suffering. He refused to let depression break him, but rather used it to make him stronger. Thus he became just the kind of man the nation needed in the moments of its greatest peril, and was transformed in the minds of its grateful citizens from a mortal creature of flesh and blood and bone into the marble god of democracy who smiles down on all that visit his temple on the mall in Washington D. C.

BIBLIOGRAPHY

Abraham Lincoln, The Prairie Years and the War Years. Carl Sandburg, Harcourt Brace and World. 1926 (CSPY, CSWY)

Abraham Lincoln, A Documentary Portrait Through His Speeches and Writings. Don E. Fehrenbacher. The New American Library of Literature. 1964 (ALDP)

Herndon's Informants, Letters, Interviews and Statements About Abraham Lincoln. Douglas L. Wilson, Rodney O. Davis. University of Illinois Press. 1998(HI)

Herndon's Lincoln; The True Story of a Great Life. Da Capo Press, Chicago. 1983 (HL)

Honor's Voice, The Transformation of Abraham Lincoln. Alfred A. Knopf. 1998 (HV)

Life On The Circuit With Lincoln. Henry Clay Whitney. (LCL)

Lincoln. David Herbert Donald. Simon and Schuster. 1995

Lincoln's Battles With God, A President's Struggle With Faith and What It Meant For America. Stephen Mansfield. Thomas Nelson Press. 2012 (LBG)

Lincoln Day By Day, A Chronology. Earl Scheck Meirs, William B. Barringer. Morningside House. 1991 (LDBD)

Lincoln and Medicine. Glenna R. Schroeder-Lein. Southern Illinois University Press. 2012 (L and M)

Lincoln's Melancholy. Joshua Wolf Schenck. Houghton Mifflin Company. 2005 (LM)

Lincoln's New Salem. Benjamin P. Thomas. Abraham Lincoln Bookshop. 1954 (LNS)

Lincoln's Unknown Private Life: An Oral History by His Black Housekeeper. Mariah Vance, 1850-1860. Lloyd Ostendorf, Walter Olesky. Hastings House Book Publishing. 1995 (LUPL)

Lincoln's Virtues, An Ethical Biography. William E. Miller, Alfred A. Knopf. 2002 (LV)

Lincoln's Youth, Indiana Years. Louis A. Warren, 1816-1830. Indiana Historical Society. 1959 (LY)

Mary Todd Lincoln, A Biography. Jean H. Baker, W. W. Norton Company. 1997 (MTL)

Mrs. Lincoln, A Life. Catherine Clinton. Harper Collins. 2009(Mrs. L)

The Complete Writings of Thomas Paine. Volume One. Phillip S. Foner. Citadel Press, New York. 1945

The Inner World of Abraham Lincoln. Michael Burlingame. University of Illinois Press, 1994 (IWL)

The Life of Abraham Lincoln. Ward Hill Lamon. University of Nebraska Press. 1999 (LAM)

The Life of Lincoln. Volume One. Ida Tarbell. Lincoln Historical Society. 1900 (IT)

The Shadows Rise, Abraham Lincoln and the Ann Rutledge Legend. John E. Walsh. University of Illinois Press. 1993 (SR)

Washington In Lincoln's Time. Noah Brooks. New York, The Century Company. 1895 (WLT)

With Malice Toward None. Stephen Ambrose. Harper and Rowe. 1977 (MTN)

FOOTNOTES

Any material quoted more than once is referred to by the abbreviation listed at the end of its entry in the bibliography.

INTRODUCTION

1. Stephen Mansfield, *Lincoln's Battle With God, A President's Struggle With Faith And What It Meant For America* (Thomas Nelson, 2012), 10

2. Joshua Wolf Schenk, *Lincoln's Melancholy*, (Houghton Mifflin Company, 2005), 12

3. LM, 12

4. LM, 12

5. LBG, 2

CHAPTER ONE- BACKWOODS BOYHOOD

1. Tarbell, Ida, *The Life Of Lincoln*, Volume One (Lincoln History Society, New York, 1900), 14

2. LM, 15

3. Carl Sandburg, *Abraham Lincoln, The Prairie Years*, Volume One (Harcourt, Brace and World, 1926), 15

4. CSPY, Volume One, 16

5. CSPY, Volume One, 16

6. CSPY, Volume One, 16

7. CSPY, Volume One, 16

8. CSPY, Volume One, 19

9. CSPY, Volume One, 65

10. Wilson, Douglas L., Davis, Rodney O., *Herndon's Informants - Letters, Interviews And Statements About Abraham Lincoln* (University of Illinois Press, 1998), 234

11. HI, 557

12. HI, 676

13. HI, 676

14. IT, 15

CHAPTER TWO - CROSSING THE OHIO

1. Warren, Louis A., *Lincoln's Youth, Indiana Years 1816-1830* (Indiana Historical Society, 1959)

2. Michael Burlingame, *The Inner World Of Abraham Lincoln* (University of Illinois Press, 1994), 22

3. Earl Schenk Meirs, William B. Barringer, *Lincoln Day By Day, A Chronology* (Morningside House, 1991), 6

4. LY, 20

5. LY, 20

6. LY, 21

7. HI, 37

8. CSPY, Volume One, 32

9.

10. HI, 39

11. LY, 52

12. LY, 54

13. LY, 56

14. Ward H. Lamon, *The Life Of Abraham Lincoln*, (University of Nebraska Press, 1999), 31

15. LAM, 41

16. LAM, 43

17. LAM, 41

18. LAM, 40

19. LAM, 37

20. LY, 48

21. LY, 47

22. LY, 47

23. HI, 131

24. LY, 137

25. LY, 173

26. LY, 173

CHAPTER THREE – RIVER MAN

1. LY, 179

2. LY, 180

3. LY, 180-181

4. CSPY, Volume One, 88

5. Reported by Absalom Gentry, son of Allen Gentry, who claimed he heard his father say it, then related to Mrs. Bess V. Ehrmann, who wrote of it in a letter held by the Lincoln National Life Foundation.

6. HI, 118

7. LY, 190

8. LY, 200

9. LY, 201

10. LY, 201

11. LY, 203

12. LY, 207

13. LY, 209

CHAPTER FOUR –COMING OF AGE

1. LY,203

2. LY, 207

3. LDBD, 13, 14

4. LAM, 78

5. HI, 13

6. LDBD,14

7. Benjamin P. Thomas, *Lincoln's New Salem*, (Abraham Lincoln Bookshop, 1954), 59

8. CSPY, Volume One, 110

9. CSPY, Volume One, 110

10. LAM, 39

11. CSPY, Volume One, 111

CHAPTER FIVE – IN SEARCH OF A FUTURE

1. CSPY, Volume One, 136

2. CSPY, Volume One, 136

3. CSPY, Volume One, 137

4. LNS, 74

5. CSPY, Volume One, 151

6. LNS, 79

7. LNS, 83

8. LNS, 85

9. LNS, 85

10. LNS, 86

11. LDBD, 34

12. HI, 556

CHAPTER SIX- ANN RUTLEDGE, ROMANCE OR RUMOR?

1. John E. Walsh, *The Shadows Rise*, Abraham Lincoln and the Ann Rutledge Legend, University of Illinois Press, 1993, 28

2. SR, 28

3. SR, 28

4. HI, 604

5. HI, 403

6. LDBD, 34

7. William Herndon, *Herndon's Lincoln: The True Story of a Great Life*, Belford and Clark, Chicago, 1899, reprinted by Da Capo Press, New York, 1983, 105-115

8. HI, 557

9. HI, 440

10. SR, 40

11. SR, 40

CHAPTER SEVEN – LOSS, LOVE THE LEGISLATURE AND LAW

1. CSPY, 190

2. LDBD, 50

3. Phillip S. Foner, *The Complete Writings of Thomas Paine*, Volume One, Citadel Press, New York, 1945, 464

4. HI, 472

5. Douglas Wilson, Honor's Voice, *The Transformation of Abraham Lincoln*, Alfred A. Knopf, 1998, 125

6. HV, 126

7. HV, 138

8. HV, 138

9. HV, 132

10. HV, 132

11. HV, 132

12. HV, 137

13. Don E. Fehrenbacher, *Abraham Lincoln: A Documentary Portrait Through His Speeches and Writings*, The New American Library of Literature, 1964, 35-36

14. LM, 44

15. LM, 40

16. LM, 41

CHAPTER EIGHT – FINDING HIS PATH

1. Jean H. Baker, *Mary Todd Lincoln, A Biography*, W. W. Norton Company, 1987, 51

2. Catherine Clinton, *Mrs. Lincoln, A Life*, Harper Collins, 2009, 44

3. MTL, 85

4. MTL, 85

5. Mrs. L, 45

6. Mrs. L, 40

7. Mrs. L, 49

8. HI, 133

9. HI, 474

10. LM, 57

11. MTL, 91

12. MTL, 91

13. MTL, 91

14. LM, 58, 59

15. HI, 431

16. HL, 259

17. LM, 62

18. LM, 62

19. MTL, 92

20. ALDP, 46

21. LDBD, 167

22. Mrs. L, 56

23. LDBD, 175

24. Mrs. L., 56

25. ALDP, 50

26. MTL, 95

27. MTL, 95

28. MTL, 97

CHAPTER NINE– HUSBAND, FATHER, CANDITATE

1. MTL, 100

2. CSPY, Volume One, 293

3. LDBD, 202

4. LDBD, 201

5. LDBD, 205

6. CSPY, Vol. One, 293

7. Glenna R. Schroeder-Lein, *Lincoln and Medicine*, Southern Illinois University Press, 2012, 10

8. Mrs. L, 67

9. MTL, 104

10. LDBD, 227

11. LDBD, 243

12. LDBD, 257

13. ALDP, 52, 53

14. LDBD, 262

15. LDBD, 268

16. LM, 120, 121

17. LM, 123

18. LBG, 64, 65

19. LM, 124

20. LDBD, 291

21. LDBD, 295

CHAPTER TEN- CONGRESSMAN LINCOLN

1. CSPY, V. 1,366

2. LDBD, 300

3. LDBD, 303

4. CSPY, V. 1, 357

5. Mrs. L, 83

6. Mrs. L, 83

7. LDBD, 319

8. LDBD, 320

9. LDBD, 322

10. LDBD, 322

11. LDBD, 323, 324

12. LDBD, 326

13. LDBD, 1849-1860, 3

CHAPTER ELEVEN – EARNING A LIVING

1. CSPy, V.1, 406

2. LDBD, 1849-1860, 13

3. LDBD, 1849-1860, 16

4. MTL, 124

5. CSPY, V. 1, 419

6. CSPY, V. 1, 419

7. CSPY, V.1, 416

8. LDBD, 1849-1860, 59

9. LDBD, 1849-1860, 63

10. LDBD, 1849-1860, 63

CHAPTER TWELVE - OUT OF THE WILDERNESS

1. CSPY, V.2, 5

2. LDBD, 1849-1860, 127

3. CSPY, V.2, 9

4. CSPY, V.2, 11

5. CSPY, V.2, 11

6. CSPY, V.2, 12

7. CSPY, V.2, 16

8. CPY, V.2, 18

9. CSPY, V.2, 19

10. LDBD, 1849-1860, 131

11. CSPY, V.2, 20

12. MTL, 150

13. LDBD, 1849-1860, 153

14. CSPY, V.2, 22-23

15. Henry Clay Whitney, *Life on the Circuit With Lincoln*, 80

16. LDBD, 1849-1860, 190

17. LDBD, 1849-1860, 205

18. LDBD, 1849-1860, 207

19. LDBD, 1849-1860, 217

20. Mrs. L., 107

21. LM, 98

22. CSPY, V.2, 168

23. CSPY, V.2, 170

24. LDBD, 1849-1860, 248

25. LDBD, 1849-1860, 268

26. LDBD, 1849-1860, 277

27. LDBD, 1849-1860, 284

28. LDBD, 1849-1860, 287

29. LDBD, 1849-1860, 294

30. CSPY, V.2, 368

CHAPTER THIRTEEN - INTO THE FIERY FURNACE

1. Noah Brooks, *Washington in Lincoln's Time*, New York: The Century Company, 1895, 220-222

2. LM, 171

3. ALDP, 160

4. LM, 176

5. ALDP, 162-163

6. IWAL, 104

7. Stephen Ambrose, With Malice Toward None, Harper and Rowe, 1977, 264

8. Mrs. L., 165

9. Mrs. L, 167

10. ALDP, 192

11. ML, 332

12. ML, 340

13. LM, 205

14. LM, 205

15. David Herbert Donald, *Lincoln*, Simon and Schuster, 1995, 549

16. *Lincoln*, 548

17. ALDP, 268

18. HI, 157, 158

19. L & M, 32, 33

20. LBG, 181-185

21. MTL, 241

22. MTN, 425-426

23. LM, 209

24. CSWY, V.4, 265

CHAPTER FOURTEEN – DEALING WITH THE DARKNESS

1. LBG, 14-15

2. HI, 499

3. LM,117

4. HI, 396

5. HI,190

6. LM, 115

7. LM,115

8. LNS,13

9. HI, 358

10. LBG, 120

11. LBG, 120

12. LBG, 122

13. L&M,14-16

William Kolasinski

ABOUT THE AUTHOR

Bill Kolasinski lives with his wife Sue in Elgin, Illinois, near his two daughters and their families. Retired after a 40 year career in sales, he finally has the free time to write about his passions, Abraham Lincoln and the Civil War era. His first book, "Glory To Grave, The Not So Ordinary Lives Of Nine Civil War Notables" was published in 2016 and is available on Amazon, as is his newest book, "A. Lincoln, A Life In The Shadow Of Death." He is currently at work on his third book and hopes to complete it in 2018.